LEADING
WITH
PURPOSE

A Leadership Framework for non-Native
School Leaders Serving in Predominately Native
Schools

Dr. Ralph M. Watkins, Ph.D.

For information, please contact:

Ralph M. Watkins

90 Glengate Loop Cathlamet, WA 98612

rwatkins@empoweredvoicesorg.org

ISBN: 978-1-970435-20-7

Published By; Ink Founders

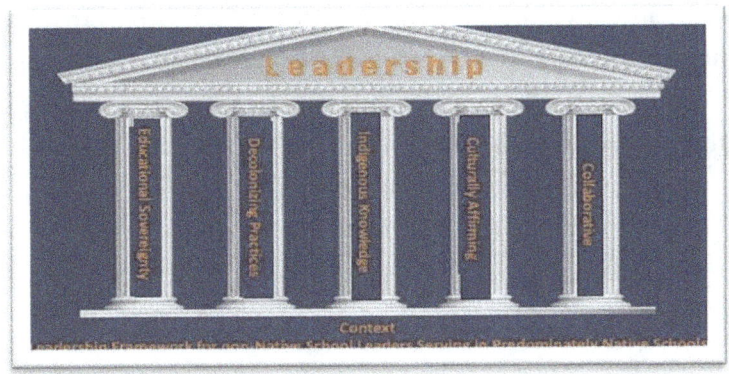

Illustrated by Dr. Ralph M. Watkins

This graphic helps conceptualize the leadership framework for non-Native school leaders serving in predominantly Native schools. It should be noted and understood that this structure sits upon context. All leadership, especially Native leadership, is contextual. Each Native community, tribe, and people is different. Knowing and understanding the context of your leadership is critical. The roof of the structure represents the overall idea of leadership: leading with honor and guiding and directing work in ways that acknowledge Indigenous cultures and values.

Taken as a whole, the graphic suggests that one does not lead predominantly Native schools alone but rather with the support of these pillars. Each of these pillars represents essential dispositions for the leader to lead effectively with respect and humility. The design and symbolism of each pillar emphasize the interdependent nature of these dispositions, further demonstrating that a practical, respectful leadership approach requires the simultaneous operation of all five pillars. These pillars strongly support that roof and represent authentic leadership, where a good relationship with Indigenous communities is based on understanding, respect, and collaboration.

The leadership framework depicted in this graphic serves as a powerful metaphor for the work of non-Native school leaders. It

3

represents intentional leadership in spaces filled with Native culture and life, cultivating and nurturing an existence congruent with practice, purpose, and goodwill. This metaphor underscores the depth and complexity of the role of a non-Native school leader in a predominantly Native school.

Land Acknowledgment

As the author of "Leading with Purpose" and a resident of Angoon, Alaska, I am profoundly grateful and humbled to live and work on the ancestral lands of the Tlingit people of Angoon. As I continue to benefit from the resources and beauty of this land, I acknowledge the sacrifices and resilience of the Tlingit people of Angoon, who have faced and overcome immense challenges while continuing to protect and celebrate their sovereignty, culture, and traditions. This acknowledgment comes from a place of deep respect and gratitude for the Tlingit community and their enduring presence and stewardship.

– Dr. Ralph M. Watkins

Dedication

This book is dedicated to the Indigenous peoples of Alaska, with whom I have had the immense honor of serving as a school leader. My gratitude to these communities knows no bounds; they have shown me how to move forward and have proven to be worthy partners and better neighbors in their struggle for educational sovereignty. The vibrant traditions of these cultures have provided invaluable knowledge and experience integral to the fundamentals detailed in this text.

To my wife, Jolene Watkins, thank you for supporting me throughout this long journey. Your support, strength, patience, and encouragement have allowed me to approach this work with a whole heart and an open mind.

This book is also dedicated to Heather Lgeik'i Powell, whom I am fortunate to call my sister. We are not connected by blood; our love for the Tlingit people unites us for all eternity. Our shared commitment to the revitalization of Tlingit culture and our dedication to future generations bind us in a pursuit larger than ourselves.

I stand in solidarity with Alaska Native people and pledge to honor them through cultural and educational recognition, among other efforts. May the common ground this book represents be one we all share and, more importantly, may it serve as a tool for those wishing to collaborate.

My Personal Introduction

It was a long time ago, about 44 years, when, in 1979, I was an energetic young student at John C. Fremont High School in Los Angeles. Picture a beautiful sunny day on the quad, and me watching four students perform a cappella with such skill that their voices could rival The Beatles on their best day. Their four-part harmonies drew a crowd of students, myself included. As a crooner, I was naturally attracted to their tune, and before I realized it, I started singing along.

The Fountain Incident

Now, keep in mind that I wasn't Luther Vandross. I may not have known all the words to their songs, nor could I define the harmonic arrangements, but that didn't stop me. I stuck to them like glue for a week, attempting to sing along. Then, one day at the fountain in the center of the quad, one of those singers, who would become one of my very best friends, kicked me into the fountain without skipping a note of his song. I emerged soaked and confused, but I got the message: I probably needed to stop trying to sing along.

The Apology and the Lesson

A week later, the fountain-kicker approached me, apologized, and dropped a wisdom bomb that would stick with me. He said, "It's not that you sounded like a cat in a blender, but you were messing up our groove. You didn't know the music or the parts. The idea is if you want to sing along with us, learn the fucking songs." So, I did. I practiced with them daily, learned the songs and harmonies, and we were best friends and a band for years.

7

The Moral of the Story

What is the takeaway from this watery, racy story? Avoid inserting yourself into an already established schedule, culture, or way of doing something, expecting that you already understand. You must learn the ropes and understand the system; only then can you fit in. This book builds on this story.

Implications for non-Native School Leaders

This principle is especially applicable to non-Native school leaders in predominantly Native schools. It's not merely about showing up and starting to sing your song. First, learn the culture and respect the process, then try to sing along with their songs. That is the only way you can contribute to the community and be a part of its harmony. The framework introduced in this book is designed to help non-Native school leaders learn the songs of the communities they serve, ensuring they support rather than cause further harm.

Preface

Significant progress has been made to enhance the success of Indigenous students. Using strategies such as place-based and experiential learning, culturally relevant curricula, and community engagement. Motivated by these efforts to address historical legacies and systemic racism, notable advancements have been achieved over the past 20 years. While graduation rates for students identifying as American Indians/Alaska Natives (AIAN) have improved nationally (National Center for Educational Statistics [NCES], 2019), the persistent academic performance gaps between AIAN and white students underscore the need for continued focus on educational equity for Indigenous communities.

Although researchers like John Hattie have explored the role of school leaders, the role of non-Native school leaders in predominantly Native schools has been largely overlooked. This book aims to address this gap by presenting a leadership framework based on five critical pillars to help non-Native leaders navigate the complexities of leading in these predominantly Native spaces. These pillars emphasize foundational dispositions, such as respect and understanding, and the integration of Indigenous perspectives into educational leadership for effective engagement. They include: gaining knowledge and appreciating Native educational sovereignty; decolonizing leadership practices; broadening the teaching of Indigenous knowledge beyond isolated curricular experiences; transitioning from cultural responsiveness to culturally affirming practices that celebrate Native identity; and moving toward genuine co-construction of decision-making with Native stakeholders.

This book will elaborate on each of these areas with examples and practical solutions, enabling non-Native leaders to better support the healing of Native students in their schools and to take responsibility for ongoing decolonization efforts. This framework addresses current educational gaps and fosters educational leadership that respects and actively promotes Indigenous rights and perspectives in education.

Key Terms

Academic Performance Gaps:

Disparities in the educational performance between groups of students, particularly those defined by socioeconomic status, race/ethnicity, and gender.

Affirming Native Identity:

Recognizing, supporting, and celebrating the unique cultural identities of Native students within educational settings.

Co-construction of Decision-Making:

A collaborative process in which leaders and stakeholders jointly make decisions, ensuring that all voices are heard and valued.

Community Engagement:

The process of working collaboratively with community groups to address issues that impact the well-being of those groups.

Cultural Identity Preservation:

Efforts to maintain and protect the cultural identities of a group, especially in the face of external pressures and changes.

Cultural Nuances:

Subtle differences in expression, views, or responses specific to a particular culture.

Cultural Responsiveness:

The ability to learn from and relate respectfully to people of one's own culture and those from other cultures.

Culturally Relevant Curricula:

Educational content is designed to reflect the backgrounds, languages, and cultures of the students it serves, making learning more engaging and effective.

Decolonizing Leadership Practices:

Efforts to recognize and eliminate colonial influences and biases in leadership styles and practices, particularly in education.

Experiential Learning:

A process through which students develop knowledge, skills, and values from direct experiences outside of a traditional academic setting.

Healing of Native Students:

Efforts aimed at addressing and alleviating psychological and emotional damage caused by historical and ongoing injustices faced by Native students.

Historical Legacies:

The lasting effects of past events and actions, particularly how they influence current circumstances and perceptions.

Indigenous Cultures:

The customs, social practices, and cultural beliefs of Indigenous peoples.

Indigenous Knowledge:

Local knowledge Indigenous cultures hold about various aspects of life, including philosophy, medicine, and the environment.

Indigenous Rights and Perspectives:

The inherent rights of Indigenous peoples are derived from their political, legal, and cultural traditions.

Leadership Framework:

A structured set of concepts and principles that guide leaders' actions and behaviors within an organization.

Native Educational Sovereignty:

The right of Native peoples to control their educational systems and processes, including the content and delivery of education.

non-Native School Leaders:

School leaders who do not identify as members of Indigenous or Native communities but work in schools that serve predominantly Indigenous populations.

Place-Based Learning:

An educational approach that uses the local community and environment as a starting point to teach concepts in language arts, mathematics, social studies, science, and other subjects.

Predominantly Native Schools:

Educational institutions where most of the student population is Native.

Reflective Practices:

Methods and techniques that help individuals and groups reflect on their behavior and performance to improve learning and outcomes.

Systemic Barriers:

Institutionalized policies and practices that create disadvantages for certain groups of people.

Systemic Racism:

Forms of racism that are embedded as everyday practices within society or an organization, leading to discrimination in areas such as criminal justice, employment, housing, health care, political power, and education.

Transformative Leadership:

A leadership style in which leaders and followers work together to elevate morale and motivation.

Tribal Involvement:

The active participation of tribal communities in planning, developing, and implementing policies and programs that affect their members, particularly in education.

Tribal Engagement:

Engaging with tribal entities and members to ensure their perspectives and needs are considered in decision-making processes related to education and community development.

Introduction

Significant effort has been dedicated to improving outcomes for Native students. These initiatives encompass place-based and experiential learning, culturally relevant curriculum, community and tribal involvement, professional development, teacher recruitment, and addressing issues of racism and historical legacies. While these efforts have achieved some success, there is still much work to be done.

According to the National Center for Educational Statistics, over the past 20 years, AIAN students have made gains in crucial educational areas, including higher academic attainment and improved graduation rates. However, gaps in academic performance between AIAN and white students remain. Closing these gaps and enhancing educational outcomes for Indigenous students is a global priority.

This book aims to explore an under-researched area: the role of school leadership, specifically that of non-Native school leaders serving predominantly Native schools. It seeks to provide a framework for non-Native school leaders, including insights, case studies, and practical strategies to navigate the complexities of working in predominantly Native environments.

The framework for non-Native school leaders in predominantly Native schools emphasizes five critical areas of leadership necessary for effective engagement in these contexts. These areas include the leader's ability to demonstrate, understand, and embrace Native educational sovereignty; actively work to decolonize their leadership practices; and prioritize Indigenous knowledge in ways that extend beyond mere curricular inclusion to influence how school leadership is enacted. The framework encourages leaders to move from cultural responsiveness to cultural affirmation, recognizing and celebrating Native identities. Furthermore, authentic collaboration with Native stakeholders fosters shared decision-making and acknowledges the impact of colonization.

Before implementing this framework, school leaders must recognize the need for a paradigm shift grounded in an understanding of how colonization has shaped the trajectory of Native populations.

The Impact of Colonization

The effects of colonization have been, and continue to be, far-reaching and long-lasting, particularly in education. For instance, in Southern Africa, before the arrival of European colonists, education was deeply embedded in community life among the Khoi, San, and Bantu-speaking peoples. To meet the expectations of colonizers, the community-focused approach had to become more formal, shifting the emphasis to the transmission of cultural knowledge, traditions, stories, and rituals from adults to children. Education was not different from daily life: it encompassed social, cultural, aesthetic, religious, and entertaining activities. Understanding the magnitude of this drastic transformation requires examining the characteristics of pre-colonial education systems alongside a critical analysis of the colonial education system in the West and its lasting repercussions for Indigenous communities.

Indigenous Schooling in Pre-Colonial Times

Before colonization, Native education was closely tied to the culture, society, and environment of indigenous people, each exhibiting unique characteristics.

Nature-Based and Collectivist:

Indigenous education was holistic, relying on spiritual, cultural, and practical learning. Such methods ensured that cultural values, traditions, and skills remained applicable to the community's needs.

Informal and Experiential:

Education among Indigenous groups tended to be less formal, delivered through storytelling, oral traditions, and experience. Elders and community members of their generation shared knowledge long before the term "education" was coined, knowledge that was essential for life and provided practical skills for all.

Integration of Learning with Environment and Culture:

Education was intertwined with the environment and culture, encompassing knowledge of local ecosystems, social systems, and cultural practices, including art, music, and crafts.

Learning Together and Collaboration:

The learning experience was collaborative and community-based, fostering cooperation and a sense of belonging, with shared responsibility for the community.

Spiritual and Moral Development:

The most important aspects of the spiritual lessons were moral development, the recognition that people and life exist in spheres beyond Earth, and the highlighting of the role individuals play in maintaining harmony with nature.

The Colonial Paradigm Shift

One aim of colonial education was to assimilate Indigenous peoples by transforming their knowledge and practices into Western values and norms. Despite this, Indigenous cultures have demonstrated remarkable resilience, adapting to changes while preserving their unique identities. A significant aspect of this process was the shift in language and curriculum; the colonizer's language became the medium of instruction, circulating Western ideologies and contributing to the loss of Native cultures. Even when Native knowledge was integrated, it was rarely the focus of curricula, which predominantly centered on Western history, science, and literature.

The Western education model also stresses individualism and competition among students, which allows them to shine as individuals through grades, marks, and examinations. This starkly contrasts with Indigenous education, which focuses on the power of community.

Western approaches rely heavily on subjects such as mathematics, science, and technology, which have contributed to economic growth and global dominance. However, these approaches often overlook the value of Indigenous knowledge systems, which offer vital insights into local ecosystems and sustainability. Recognizing and valuing these knowledge systems is essential for creating a more holistic approach to education and sustainability.

The Western educational model is teacher-centric, positioning the teacher as both a repository of knowledge and the sole authority for imparting it. In contrast, Indigenous educational systems view teachers as mentors who guide students rather than dictate what they should know. This positionality represents a key philosophical difference between Indigenous and Western education. Consequently, Native students must navigate a world that frequently undermines their knowledge and values.

While Western education focuses on individual success, the influence of corporations, standardized structures, and top-down governance has eroded much of our shared heritage. In contrast, Indigenous knowledge systems emphasize the importance of diverse identities grounded in community responsibility and universal values. Education must rise to the challenge of Indigenous knowledge by valuing and reintegrating it into today's educational framework. By doing so, we can create a more inclusive and equitable system that honors diverse perspectives and fosters a deeper understanding of global interdependence. Instead of ignoring the cultural differences that shape our students' tastes and belief systems, we should encourage them to incorporate Native educational techniques, which will enhance their academic experience and promote a world in which all cultures are recognized and appreciated.

Conflicts and Consequences

Western education paradigms were hardly free of conflict, and some consequences have been dire for Indigenous communities.

Loss of Culture:

The emphasis on Western knowledge has led to a decline in the use of local languages and the erosion of embedded cultural practices.

Loss of Cultural Identity and Community:

Education led to a fragmented cultural identity and a divide within the community. Many Indigenous peoples educated in Western systems suffered from alienation and identity crises, not fitting into either culture.

Continued Socioeconomic Disparities:

The impact of this change led to exacerbated disparities, as many Indigenous peoples face higher rates of poverty, unemployment, and poor health, further perpetuated by the failure of boarding schools to equip students with skills relevant to a Western-dominated world.

Intergenerational Trauma:

For example, the intent behind the residential school system in Canada was to eliminate the Indigenous population through forced integration. These schools sought to assimilate Indigenous children by removing them from their families, prohibiting their languages, and normalizing Euro-Canadian and Christian ways of life, resulting in extensive abuse, neglect, and intergenerational trauma.

The process of colonization brought immense transformation to Indigenous education, replacing holistic, community-based systems with formal, Western-oriented models that largely disregarded or eroded Indigenous values, knowledge, and structures. This transition devastated local cultures and placed significant strain on the social balance of precolonial societies.

Current Reality of Colonization's Impact

Globally, colonization led to a consistent undermining of

Indigenous peoples, resulting in a routine lack of recognition of their Native sovereignties, particularly regarding their rights to self-determination and education. Educational sovereignty has been stripped from Native peoples and replaced with a system that has failed to educate many Native students, depriving them of their language, culture, and identities.

In the United States, approximately 459,000 AIAN students are enrolled in kindergarten through Grade 12. Most of these students, about 93%, or 427,00, attend regular public schools. In comparison, around 7% (34,529 students) are enrolled in schools operated or funded by the Federal Bureau of Indian Education (National Center for Education Statistics, 2023).

The educational landscape for AIAN students reveals that nearly 46% attend rural schools, reflecting the geographical distribution of Indigenous populations across the country. A notable portion of these students, approximately 265,912, attend schools where 50% or more of the student body identifies as AIAN.

These statistics highlight the unique educational experiences and challenges faced by Native students, underscoring the importance of understanding their demographics to improve academic outcomes and develop support systems tailored to their needs.

Systemic issues further challenge the educational experiences of Native students enrolled in public schools, which are often located in the most impoverished areas of their respective states. This results in a lack of funding and resources. In 2019, Ed Build, a nonprofit organization that studies school funding, released a report revealing significant funding disparities between predominantly white and nonwhite schools. Nationally, predominantly white school districts receive $23 billion more than their non-white counterparts, despite serving a similar number of children (Taie & Goldring, 2020).

Non-white school districts receive $2,226 less per student than white districts. This funding disparity is exacerbated by the reliance on local property taxes for school funding, perpetuating community wealth disparities in education. Schools in impoverished areas often lack the resources to provide essential services, such as counseling and mental health support, which can further compound the challenges faced by Native students.

One of the many systemic problems impacting outcomes for AIAN students is poverty. Historically, Native American children have experienced higher poverty rates than their non-Hispanic white peers. In 2022, more than 1 in 4 (25.9%) AIAN children fell below the supplemental poverty line (United Way of the National Capital Area, 2023).

Students living in poverty often start school lacking the fundamental building blocks for learning.

Many governments recognize that systemic issues create seemingly insurmountable challenges for Native students and are enacting legislation to address these disparities. In 2021, Canada passed the United Nations Declaration on the Rights of Indigenous Peoples Act, reaffirming Indigenous peoples' right to establish, operate, and control schools where they can teach students in their Native languages and in ways that reflect their cultural teaching and learning methods. In Australia, the Voice to Parliament bill was introduced in 2023, signifying Indigenous sovereignty, particularly within the education sector, for many communities, schools, and Indigenous groups. The United States has a long history of attempting to address challenges affecting Native education. One landmark piece of legislation, passed in 1975, was the Indian Self-Determination and Education Assistance Act.

This legislation marked a shift in how the U.S. government recognized Indigenous peoples, moving away from the previous Termination Policy, which did not acknowledge Native sovereignty. Legislation also created greater autonomy for tribes in managing resources, fostering economic growth, and, importantly, in the education of Native children. The Education Amendments Act of 1978 was designed to provide direct funding to tribally operated schools. The Tribally Controlled Schools Act, passed in 1988, reinforced tribes' authority to create, control, and govern schools and provided greater flexibility in educational programs.

To support these efforts, non-Native leaders must recognize that colonization has a persistent impact both outside of schools and within our systems, influencing attitudes, policies, and practices. Its far-reaching effects continue to shape the education and understanding of Native students. What is needed from these leaders is a recognition that drives their motivation to take necessary actions, rather than serving as a tool that distorts and deforms Native culture further. This perspective includes adopting a new model centered on Indigenous knowledge that is genuinely collaborative, as well as affirming the cultural identity of Native students, ensuring they are not exploited in a system designed to undermine Native culture.

Framing the Conversation Around non-Native Leadership in Predominantly Native Schools

Before discussing the need for non-Native school leaders in predominantly Native schools and their critical role, the reader should acknowledge three key points. First, the colonization and subsequent subjugation of Indigenous peoples were wrong and led to the near destruction of once-thriving cultures. Second, Native people never surrendered their sovereignty and are, therefore, unconditionally entitled to it. Lastly, without colonization, we can envision a vastly different trajectory for Native peoples. Indigenous communities would have continued to thrive within their rich cultural, social, and economic systems, maintaining their traditional governance structures and ways of life, including their educational systems. These understandings frame our discussion about non-Native leadership in predominantly Native spaces.

Importance of non-Native Leadership in Predominantly Native Schools

Representation

A significant reason for the need for non-Native school leaders is the small number of available Native school leaders. The research report does not specify the percentage of American school leaders of Native ancestry, and, based on the existing data, this is a deficiency. In 2021, approximately 78.4% of school principals in the U.S. were white, 8.7% were Hispanic or Latino, 9.5% were African American, and 1.3% were Asian. AIAN leaders constituted only 0.7% (National Center for Education Statistics, 2022).

The Lack of American Indian and Alaska Native Leaders in Public Education

Several factors contribute to the stark inequalities faced by AIAN students in today's educational system, with the Native leadership deficit being a significant concern. This demographic reality raises questions about who leads these schools and what this lack of representation means for students. It also presents challenges for teachers, who may not see educators who resemble them at various stages of their careers.

Understanding the Context

To grasp the extent of the representation gaps, consider some statistics. According to the National Center for Educational Statistics (2019), the average rural school has 365 students. Based on the 2007-2008 percentage distribution of public elementary and secondary students by race/ethnicity and locale, published by the National Center for Educational Statistics,

There are 249,322 AIAN students enrolled in rural schools in the U.S., which would require 658 individual schools.

Suppose we estimate the number of school districts, assuming an average of five schools per district. In that case, we arrive at a more conservative estimate of 132 school districts where the predominant population is AIAN. To summarize, we hypothesize that dividing the 249,322 AIAN students into 658 schools, each with an enrollment of 365, would be optimal. Next, by creating school districts comprising 5 ~~schools~~ each, we divide 658 schools by 5, yielding 132 school districts. With one principal per-school and one superintendent per district, we estimate approximately 790 administrators in this hypothetical scenario.

The Administrative Landscape

With 790 administrators across an estimated 132 districts, an administrative hierarchy usually consists of one superintendent and one principal per school. Fewer than 0.07% identify as AIAN.

This statistic means that only 46 of the 658 principals in these public schools with a dominant AIAN population were themselves

AIAN. Only 9 of the 132 superintendents are AIAN. This trend is especially troubling considering that most of those schools are majority Native student–populated. Proximity and shared lived experiences between educators and students are, of course, ideal. Still, the fact is that in most schools today, many leaders who make decisions do not look like their students or share similar histories.

Why Underrepresentation Takes a Toll

This level of underrepresentation has significant consequences. Beyond equity, diversity in leadership fosters cohesion among student demographics and administrative policyholders, leading to greater cultural competency that meets the needs of our emerging world citizens. Leaders who understand the demographics of AIAN students are crucial, as they can incorporate these specific needs into systems and frameworks rather than subsuming them under a more general narrative.

When there is insufficient representation, a school may fail to be inclusive and affirm Native identities and experiences. Hiring and developing AIAN leaders is imperative to ensure that these students are heard and their human rights are respected within educational institutions.

This gap highlights the necessity of involving non-Native school leaders in discussions about and interacting with the leadership framework for those serving predominantly Native schools. The five pillars: Educational Sovereignty, Decolonizing Leadership Practices, Indigenous Knowledge First, Culturally Affirming Leadership Practices, and Collaboration, are designed to assist non-Native leaders in navigating the unique cultural, educational, and social dynamics present in Native schools.

While the proposed framework is not a cure-all, it represents a significant step forward. The framework has the potential to bridge the gap between the student body's cultural identities and the cultural competencies of school leadership. This transformation is a promising development for an educational system that allows Native students to thrive without sacrificing their culture.

Leadership

Leadership is essential in any organization. More importantly, however, is the correct type of leadership. Having appropriate leadership applies to both business organizations and those tasked with educating children. Having the right leader guiding the right way is crucial in a school system. Understanding the context for leadership is foundational for non-Native school leaders serving in predominantly Native schools.

A renowned researcher, John Hattie, spent years studying factors affecting student learning. Hattie sought to understand more about mere chance occurrences or the statistical significance of these factors; his work focused on causes, their impact, and their relationship to change. In statistics, this is known as "effect size." Effect size is a quantitative value that measures the strength of a relationship between two variables in a given population.

In statistics, the effect size is considered low and statistically significant if it falls within the range 0 to 0.2. Noticeable or moderate significance is between 0.2 and 0.5. If an effect size is 0.80 or greater, it is considered substantial. In Hattie's book "Visible Learning," Hattie used effect size to describe the impact of factors influencing student achievement. Regarding school leadership, he found an overall effect size of 0.36, indicating moderate significance according to Cohen's scale. When examining leadership styles, Hattie found that transformational leadership, described as a dynamic, inspiring style that motivates and empowers followers to achieve a shared vision through personal growth and development, had a low effect size (0.11). Leadership characterized by reflection, collaboration, teacher empowerment, and support for self-efficacy had a high impact with a score of 0.91.

Missing from Hattie's work are data explicitly generated from studies of Native students and their unique educational environments, and from examinations of how leadership is enacted within those settings. Native students often attend schools where teachers and leaders do not share their language, culture, or worldview, how this impacts student achievement warrants further research. However, substantial research shows a positive correlation between student achievement and a shared culture among students, teachers, and leaders (Cherng & Halpin, 2016).

Leadership in Context

The leadership framework for non-Native school leaders serving in predominantly Native schools is founded on the principle that leadership occurs within a specific context. For non-Native school leaders in Native schools, this contextual concept is critical. Each Native tribe possesses a unique cultural, historical, and social framework that shapes the educational landscape, and leaders must learn to navigate this diversity. Recognizing the role of context in leadership and the distinct structures, practices, and norms of Native communities is essential for a leader's success.

Defining Context

There is no one-size-fits-all approach to effective leadership; it is inherently context-dependent. Context encompasses the situations, events, and facts that provide a comprehensive understanding of circumstances. Unfortunately, many leaders do not utilize context effectively. The cultural, historical, and social dynamics of Native tribes vary significantly across the globe, and these unique contexts are crucial when discussing the education of Native students.

Influence of Context on Leadership

Native student success and the Native educational experience are very context-bound. Specific contexts of Native school environments make them distinct and relevant. All Native tribes have their systems, practices, and norms regarding the role of schooling. Understanding this context is essential to effective leadership and community engagement. Non-Native leaders need to be aware of the different tribal contexts; if they do not, they will perpetuate cultural ignorance, and building meaningful relationships with the community will become difficult.

Challenges and Risks

Inaccurately acknowledging context can lead to harmful leadership practices that undermine students' well-being and learning. A mismatch between the community's cultural and historical nuances and those of the leadership can lead to misinterpretation and harmful practices. Leaders must immerse themselves in the Native community to which they belong by reaching out to tribal leaders, elders, and community members for advice.

Starting with Context

The cultural, historical, and social context of an Indigenous or Native community should serve as the foundation for school leaders entering a predominantly Native environment. By embracing this context, leaders can build trust, foster collaboration, and help create a responsive community for Native students and their families. Leaders need to study the specifics of their context and learn what is valued, thereby enhancing their cultural competence and inclusive leadership.

Lift Yourself Out of Context for Leadership

The first step for school leaders is to engage in cultural competency training and communicate with local tribal leaders to gain insights into the area's history and culture. Listening to and conversing with members of the Native community can inspire leadership practices and decisions appropriate to the specific context.

Creating an Environment of Trust and Collaboration

Recognizing events such as the National Day of Remembrance for Indian Boarding Schools exemplifies territorial acknowledgment and strengthens the school community. Leading predominantly Native schools involves establishing trust, valuing Indigenous peoples' perspectives, and collaborating with tribal community members to design educational systems that honor cultural traditions.

Pitfalls of Ignoring Context

Ignoring context can lead to poorly conceived policies and practices that perpetuate inequity and cultural dissonance. Without leaders who understand context, students may feel alienated and marginalized, which can negatively affect their ability to build an inclusive learning environment. To create a system that supports Native student success and well-being, leaders must understand the culture, history, and social nuances of each community.

Table Of Contents

Chapter One

The Legacy of Colonization and Its Impact on Native Education

We are the keepers of the fire, passed down from father to son for centuries untold. We are the shepherds of a way of life that puts cooperation over competition, recognizing that we are all related and that our survival depends on cooperation.

- Oren R. Lyons, Onondaga Nation Faithkeeper

History of Colonization

Colonialism was a project of territorial expansion undertaken by powerful states, often involving the resettlement of the colonizing population onto newly claimed lands and the displacement, if not eradication, of the indigenous peoples who previously inhabited those areas (Nicholls, 2011). This practice of domination led to the erosion and often complete eradication of Native cultures and languages, while simultaneously imposing the colonizers' language and cultural values on the local populations (Blakemore, 2024). Colonizers employed various rationales to justify their actions, frequently asserting that it was their legal and religious right to conquer nations they deemed barbaric or savage (Benton, 2018). These colonial efforts were often endorsed and supported by religious organizations.

In 1493, Pope Alexander VI issued one of several Papal Bulls, known as Inter Caetera, granting nations the authority to seize control of other lands, subdue their inhabitants, and convert them to Christianity (Cavedon, 2024). In this edict, Pope Alexander VI declared, "that in our times especially the Catholic faith and the

Christian religion be exalted and be everywhere increased and spread, that the health of souls be cared for and that barbarous nations be overthrown and brought to the faith itself."

A landmark legal decision by Chief Justice Marshall in 1823 codified the Papal Bulls into U.S. law. This ruling denied Indigenous peoples ownership of their lands, asserting that their presence constituted mere occupancy rather than ownership. In 1775, before American independence, the Piankeshaw Indians sold land to Thomas Johnson and a group of speculators. Thirty years later, the same land was ceded to the United States through treaties and subsequently sold to Mr. McIntosh. When a legal dispute arose between Mr. Johnson and Mr. McIntosh, the courts sided with Mr. McIntosh, arguing that the Native people lacked the right to sell the land, as that right belonged to the colonizers who "discovered" it. Justice John Marshall proclaimed that the "discovery" of America granted "exclusive title to those who made it," specifically, the European colonizers. Thus, the Piankeshaws did not own what they believed was their land, nor did any Indigenous tribe.

Recently, many religious leaders and legal scholars have denounced this doctrine. In 2023, nearly 500 years after papal decrees were used to justify Europe's colonial conquests, the Vatican repudiated these decrees, stating that the "Doctrine of Discovery," which was used to justify the suppression of Indigenous cultures and livelihoods, is not part of the Catholic faith (Chappell, 2023).

The Impact of Colonization on Native Education

There is currently no metric to measure the impact of colonization on the educational outcomes of Indigenous students. While several approaches and studies have been developed to assess these impacts, most traditional methods fail to capture the nuanced effects of colonization. Many conventional approaches overlook the cultural suppression that has led to the loss of language, traditional names, spiritual practices, and cultural ceremonies. Colonization has also rendered Native peoples more vulnerable to mental and other health issues, which, in turn, affects how Native students engage in learning environments. Most assessments used to quantify the achievement of Native students rely on tools, strategies, and outcomes that conflict with the traditional methods that Native communities used to educate their children and the learning outcomes they value.

More than 530 years have passed since Columbus arrived in North America, a period marked by conquest and subjugation. The U.S. government authorized over 1,500 wars, attacks, and raids against Indigenous peoples, the highest number of any country in the world. By the late 19th century, the U.S. shifted its focus from military conquest to cultural assimilation, making traditional cultural practices, Native languages, and ceremonies illegal (Marchiò, 2022). The absence of conventional learning practices is a continuation of the assimilation strategies employed by colonizers intent on eradicating Indigenous cultures.

Western education represents a significant departure from traditional Indigenous learning systems and reinforces an educational paradigm historically used as a tool for assimilation and cultural disruption. Native American communities developed complex learning systems that incorporated diverse skills and engaged all human senses to address physical, emotional, mental, spiritual, individual, and community needs (Cote, 2024). Colonization and the imposition of Western education disrupted traditional ways of learning and knowledge transmission. They had profound effects on the social fabric of Native communities, their well-being, and the prosperity of their societies (Leighton, 2024).

Traditional Education Approaches

The Importance of Oral Traditions and Storytelling

In conventional Native education, oral storytelling is a vital method for teaching history, cultural beliefs, and morals from one generation to the next. Children learn to listen, remember, and imagine, achieving social-emotional mastery in the process.

A Unique Learning Process: The educational methods of Indigenous peoples differ significantly from modern approaches, focusing primarily on observation and imitation. Children learn by watching and mimicking adults in their community, acquiring practical skills for daily living, such as fishing and hunting. This unique approach fosters a deep connection with nature and its surroundings.

Intergenerational Learning in Indigenous Education: Learning is deeply rooted in family and community. Parents, elders, and community members play crucial roles in teaching children, ensuring that education is relevant and aligned with community values. Elders convey their wisdom through stories, history, and experience, preserving the community's cultural heritage.

Experiential Learning in Indigenous Education: Indigenous education values experiential learning that engages students' senses and connects them to their cultural landscapes. This place-based learning approach fosters a profound connection with cultural heritage and the world around them.

Traditional Ecological Knowledge (TEK): TEK forms the core of Indigenous education, emphasizing the interconnection between living beings and ecosystems. These ancient knowledge systems have been passed down through generations, maintaining a sustainable way of life.

Cultural and Spiritual Education: Indigenous education systems incorporate teachings of culture and spirituality, often delivered through protocols, ceremonies, and traditions absent from mainstream educational practices. This approach helps learners develop a sense of identity and place, emphasizing the importance of community survival and sustainability.

Mentorship and Symbiotic Learning: Traditional Native education involves oral traditions and community enrichment through mentorship and other social structures, promoting environmental balance through symbiotic learning. These systems provide an education steeped in tradition, offering a culturally contextualized and holistic approach that has equipped Indigenous people with the tools they need to thrive for millennia.

Disparities in Achievement and Access

There is a growing trend in education to incorporate cultural elements into school curricula and practices. Various terms describe these teaching approaches, including "culturally responsive teaching," "culturally sustaining pedagogy," and the foundational "culturally relevant pedagogy." While each term has unique components defined by different researchers, they all emphasize integrating the knowledge of traditionally marginalized communities into classroom instruction (Will & Najarro, 2022). The introduction of these cultural elements is positively impacting achievement rates for American Indian and Alaska Native (AIAN) students. For example, dropout rates for AIAN students decreased from 11.5% in 2014 to 10.1% in 2017 (McFarland et al., 2020).

Despite these academic gains, the progress for AIAN students is often slow and faces sustainability challenges. Disparities between AIAN students and their white peers continue to manifest in significant ways, such as a higher likelihood of dropping out, substance abuse, and involvement with the juvenile justice system. These disparities can negatively affect the well-being of Native students.

AIAN students are twice as likely to drop out of school compared to their white counterparts, making their dropout rate the highest in the nation. This alarming statistic reflects the systemic challenges ingrained in the broader educational system (National Center for Education Statistics, 2024).

Substance abuse remains a critical issue for AIAN students, exacerbated by accessibility. In 2019, one-third (33%) of AIAN high schoolers reported using alcohol in the past month, while nearly a quarter (24%) stated that illegal drugs were available to them on school property (National Indian Education Association, 2019).

Native American youth are also disproportionately represented in the juvenile justice system, further disrupting their education. They are twice as likely as their peers to be incarcerated for minor offenses, perpetuating a cycle of recidivism. According to the Tribal Law and Policy Institute, state courts are twice as likely to incarcerate Native teens for minor crimes, such as truancy and alcohol use, compared to any other racial or ethnic group (Morales, 2015).

Disciplinary actions, including suspensions that remove Native students from the learning environment, occur at higher rates than for their non-Native peers. This pattern contributes to chronic absenteeism, alienating them from the educational system and hindering their ability to learn, thus widening the academic achievement gap between Native and non-Native students.

Native American students consistently score lower in reading and math compared to their white peers, a concerning gap that significantly predicts success in higher education and the job market. Additionally, this gap leads to a disproportionate enrollment of Native students in special education programs. Among all racial and ethnic groups, Native students are significantly more likely to be misidentified for special education, resulting in stigma, low expectations from teachers, and learning delays.

While some Native American students have made academic progress, a substantial gap remains, impacting their education, health, and overall quality of life. Native youth should be able to thrive academically, socially, and emotionally. Educational settings must challenge Native students while allowing them to maintain their cultural identity. Only through collaboration can we begin to bridge these gaps and pave the way for the success of Native American students.

Cultural Disconnection and Identity Struggles

Native students today share a legacy with millions of Native peoples who have survived colonization. While some of these survivors are thriving, many continue to grapple with the lasting effects of trauma inflicted on their ancestors. This trauma has resulted in both mental and physical challenges that affect students and contribute to academic difficulties. The loss of languages and traditions has led to cultural disconnection among Native peoples, resulting in a diminished sense of identity. This was the intended outcome of assimilation policies aimed at stripping Native children of their languages and cultural identities.

In today's educational landscape, Native students often find themselves as minorities in academic settings, lacking a strong foundation in their Native identities. This absence creates a void that is quickly filled by mainstream identities and norms. As this identity void is filled, the cultural incongruence experienced by Native students further erodes their Native identity. Consequently, many educators working with Native students may fail to recognize their unique identities, viewing them instead as part of the mainstream culture. Some argue that schools should teach non-dominant culture students their language and culture.

This argument must be reconsidered in light of the historical context of enforced assimilation and the current understanding of the importance of cultural identity. Native students should not be viewed as belonging to the mainstream culture within educational environments. Instead, teaching methods should prioritize culturally responsive education that values and integrates Native identities and traditions. This approach supports the academic and emotional well-being of Native students while enriching the learning experience for all.

For non-Native school leaders entering predominantly Native spaces, it is crucial to acknowledge that cultural incongruence is fundamental and can have lasting adverse effects on students. Leaders must intentionally implement policies and practices that reinforce Native identities.

Non-Native school leaders can serve as facilitators, supporting Native educators and community members in leadership roles, including fostering mentorship programs, professional development opportunities, and community engagement that amplify Indigenous voices. Such investments create an ecosystem that empowers Native leaders to effect change within educational systems.

Additionally, non-Native leaders should create opportunities for Native decision-making and recognize that they serve Indigenous communities. They must embrace their roles as allies and advocates for Native educational issues. To address cultural mismatches, including colonial practices that have harmed Native students, leaders should adopt practices that honor Indigenous cultural heritage and respect Indigenous frameworks (Cahill, Black, & Prout Quicke, 2022).

Moreover, implementing culturally responsive curricula, teaching methods, and assessments is vital for bridging the cultural divide between schools and Native students (Castagno & Brayboy, 2008).

These approaches affirm a student's place in the community and are essential for achieving academic growth and social progress. Non-

Native leaders should focus on building trust and acknowledging the historical trauma of Native students who were forced into boarding schools. This can be accomplished through active listening and collaboration with Indigenous communities to create an educational system that respects their knowledge and traditions.

Furthermore, culturally relevant, responsive, and relational education has been shown to enhance student engagement and success, underscoring the need to implement culturally grounded programs that encourage students and families to share their cultures and languages (Baskin, 2016).

Finally, addressing stereotypes and biases is essential for creating an equitable environment for all learners. These actions involve identifying and addressing institutional blind spots, actively working to eliminate stereotypes while maintaining high academic standards, and celebrating the talents of students and families within the school community.

Chapter Two

Pillar One: Embracing Native Peoples' Educational Sovereignty

Educational sovereignty refers to the inherent right of Indigenous tribes to define and achieve their own educational goals for their students, families, and communities (Teach for America, n.d.).

Defining Educational Sovereignty

Sovereignty, which includes the right to self-government and self-education, encompasses the rights to "linguistic and cultural expression according to local languages and norms" (Lomawaima & McCarty, 2002, p. 284). For school leaders in predominantly Native schools, especially non-Native leaders working in these spaces, grasping the concept of Native educational sovereignty is crucial. This concept serves as a guiding framework for non-Native school leaders navigating predominantly Native environments. Embracing educational sovereignty enhances school leaders' roles as capacity builders and facilitators, emphasizing the importance of respecting and integrating Indigenous ways of knowing, being, and doing into their practices. To effectively engage in this work, leaders must reflect on their biases and recognize when their behaviors or assumptions create systemic barriers for those they aim to uplift.

While there is no formal legal definition of educational sovereignty, it is generally understood as part of the broader framework of tribal sovereignty, which is recognized in legal statutes in the United States, Canada, and Australia. Educational sovereignty is a complex concept for Native American tribes, encompassing legal, cultural, and pedagogical aspects. Tribes have the fundamental right to address the historical impacts of forced assimilation by creating educational experiences that honor and celebrate their heritage, thereby taking control of their children's education. Rooted in tribal sovereignty, educational sovereignty includes the authority to design and implement culturally relevant curricula. It also encompasses the power to preserve and promote tribal languages, traditions, and cultural identities through education, as well as to govern educational systems in alignment with tribal values and needs, ensuring that Native American children receive an education that prepares them for diverse opportunities.

Leaders within Native communities have a clear understanding of their educational sovereignty and their right to it. Quinton Roman, an enrolled member of the Cheyenne and Arapaho tribes and executive director of the Tribal Education Department National Assembly, which supports AIAN tribes in their pursuit of educational sovereignty while honoring each tribe's unique spiritual and cultural traditions, stated, "Tribes were not waiting on the shores of the Atlantic for Columbus to bring us education. We have always had our means to provide instruction and education to our tribes" (Zingg, 2019). Phil Gover (Pawnee/Comanche/Paiute), who launched the Sovereign Community School in 2018, the first public charter school in Oklahoma focused on the needs of Native students in Oklahoma City, remarked, "We will not persist if we let other people who aren't us tell us what the most valuable knowledge is to carry forward to the next generation."

Importance of Supporting Native Control Over Education

Supporting Native control over education goes beyond a school leader's belief in the right to sovereignty; it is rooted in legislation. In the United States, control over education is established by laws such as the Indian Reorganization Act of 1934. This act marked a significant shift, as it was the first federal legislation requiring the teaching of Indian history and culture in Bureau of Indian Affairs (BIA) schools, moving away from previous policies aimed at erasure.

The Indian Self-Determination and Education Assistance Act of 1975 further empowered federally recognized tribes by allowing them to administer Bureau-funded schools and develop culturally relevant programs for their children. This act allocated funds to tribal schools, provided small stipends to school boards, and enabled tribes to hire local teachers. In 1978, the Education Amendments Act streamlined funding and established a direct chain of command from tribal entities to the Office of Indian Education, enhancing tribal control over educational programs.

Canada has experienced a similar progression in granting Indigenous peoples control over education. From 1972 to 2017, Canadian legislation evolved to transfer governance of education systems to Indigenous hands. While not yet achieving the ultimate goals, this journey began with the recognition of the inherent right to self-government, including authority over education as outlined in Section 35 of the Constitution Act, 1982. The Indian Control of Indian Education Policy, developed by the National Indian Brotherhood (now the Assembly of First Nations) in 1972, established local Indigenous jurisdiction over education.

In 2006, British Columbia implemented the First Nations Jurisdiction over Education in British Columbia Act, granting BC First Nations decision-making powers within their education systems. In 2014, the First Nations Control of First Nations Education Act, part of Bill C-33, became the first federal legislation to ensure Indigenous control over on-reserve education programs administered by local governing bodies.

The Anishinabek Education System, established under Ontario's 2017 Anishinabek Nation education agreement, aims to return control of educational services to many First Nations after years of federal restrictions. Recent Self-Government Agreements between Indigenous groups further enhance autonomy in education, enabling communities to provide culturally relevant programs tailored to their needs. This legislative framework has enabled Indigenous communities to develop education systems that honor the spirituality of each nation.

Legally, educational sovereignty is recognized as the right of Indigenous peoples. However, for this legislation to be effectively implemented in schools, school leaders, teachers, and staff must view its fulfillment as an obligation.

Case Study:

Navigating Leadership in a Predominantly Native School as a non-Native Educator

Introduction

As I enter my twelfth year as an educational leader in Alaska, I find myself torn between two contrasting feelings. On one hand, I have a deep passion for my profession, especially given Alaska's challenges in retaining educators and school leaders. On the other hand, I recognize that Native leadership may better serve the needs of our school community.

The Internal Conflict

This internal struggle stems from my position as a non-Native leader in a predominantly Native school. Despite my dedicated efforts to support Native educational sovereignty, implement culturally affirming leadership practices, combat marginalization, decolonize practices, create platforms for Native voices in decision-making, and advocate for Native education issues. I am aware that my non-Native identity may limit my influence.

The Research Perspective

This limitation is not a reflection of my leadership abilities or a rejection by the Native community. Research consistently shows that students from marginalized groups thrive when taught by leaders who share their race, ethnicity, and gender (Drissen, 2015; Battey et al., 2018). This research suggests that Native students could benefit even more from Native educational leaders who can relate closely to their experiences and cultural backgrounds.

The Broader Question

My situation raises a larger question in educational leadership: How can non-Native leaders best serve Native communities while creating opportunities for Native leadership to flourish? This challenge requires balancing a commitment to the community with the long-term goal of empowering Native educators to take on leadership roles.

The Dual Responsibility

In education, leadership carries significant responsibility, particularly for non-Native leaders in predominantly Native communities. These leaders are tasked not only with managing schools but also with fostering an environment in which Native populations can develop the skills and capabilities to lead their educational systems. This dual responsibility can create a complex conflict, especially when the goal of sustainability in leadership clashes with the need to empower Indigenous leadership.

The Role of Capacity Building

Central to this responsibility is the concept of capacity building. Non-native school leaders should view themselves as

~~facilitators, creating~~ pathways for Native educators and community members to assume leadership roles. This requires investing time and resources into mentorship programs, professional development, and community engagement initiatives that prioritize Indigenous voices and perspectives. By doing so, leaders can help cultivate a self-sustaining educational ecosystem that reflects the culture, values, and needs of the Native population.

Shifting the Focus

The traditional model of educational leadership often emphasizes tenure and stability, leading many superintendents to seek long tenures. However, in predominantly Native schools, the focus should shift from personal ambition to community empowerment. Non-Native leaders must adopt a service-centered mindset rather than one focused on longevity. Their goal should not be to become the longest-serving superintendent but to serve as long as there is a demonstrated need for their leadership. This perspective aligns with the broader movement toward reconciliation, emphasizing the acknowledgment of historical injustices and collaborative efforts to create equitable educational opportunities.

A Call to Action

To navigate this complex landscape, non-Native school leaders must engage in self-reflection and actively seek input from Native community members. Building trust requires listening to the needs and aspirations of Indigenous populations and collaborating with them to co-create educational frameworks that honor their cultural heritage. **Non-native leaders should approach their roles ~~with humility, recognizing~~** that their tenure in these positions is temporary and that the community's strength and resilience are the true measure of success.

Conclusion

Ultimately, the responsibility of non-Native school leaders in predominantly Native schools extends beyond basic administration; it represents an opportunity to contribute to a transformative process that enables Indigenous communities to reclaim their agency in education. By embracing this responsibility with authenticity and purpose, these leaders can help pave the way for a future where Native populations lead their educational systems, fostering an environment of empowerment, respect, and cultural revitalization.

Leadership Action Plan

There is no definitive guide for educational leaders in primarily non-Native schools to adopt Native educational sovereignty. However, certain practices and mindsets can help leaders demonstrate their understanding and commitment to this principle through training. This action plan outlines key areas for reflection and practice alignment.

At the core of this action plan is the emphasis on research and professional growth for school leaders. By engaging in focused study and Indigenous-led professional development, leaders can cultivate a comprehensive understanding of Native sovereignty. This knowledge is essential for making informed leadership decisions that respect Native educational autonomy.

Another vital component of the action plan is establishing meaningful partnerships with local Native tribes through sustained, respectful engagement. This involves dedicating time to proper introductions and relationship-building with tribal organizations to understand their educational priorities. Regular community gatherings facilitate open dialogue about academic initiatives, ensuring that tribal voices are central to school governance.

Additionally, educational leaders must integrate Native perspectives through culturally relevant curricula that honor Indigenous history, values, and ways of knowing. This requires intentional practice, training in culturally responsive pedagogy, and regular evaluation of school policies to ensure they align with the principles of Native sovereignty. Leaders should actively create pathways for Native students and community members to assume leadership roles, fostering an environment in which Indigenous voices guide educational practices and governance. These efforts should focus on developing sustainable systems that support Native educational goals while promoting authentic representation and empowerment throughout the school community.

To ensure success, ongoing monitoring and evaluation are necessary. School leaders must establish measurable goals for Native educational sovereignty through direct consultation with tribal communities. Strategic objectives should include student achievement, cultural integration, and community engagement, with regular feedback cycles to ensure programs align with the needs of Native communities. Effective leadership involves advocating for resources that support culturally grounded programming, scholarships, and professional development. Success metrics should balance academic benchmarks with community-defined indicators, prioritizing collective empowerment over individual achievement. This approach ensures that all initiatives uphold tribal sovereignty and educational self-determination while maintaining accountability to Native communities.

Tools for Reflective Growth

As you conclude this chapter, take time to reflect on the following questions, which are designed to support your personal and professional growth as a non-Native school leader. These prompts will help you assess your practices and deepen your commitment to

Indigenous educational sovereignty, decolonizing leadership, prioritizing Indigenous knowledge, culturally affirming practices, and authentic collaboration with Native communities.

Engaging thoughtfully with these questions will enhance your effectiveness as an advocate for Indigenous students and the communities you serve.

Self-Reflection Questions:

1. How do I recognize and support the right of Native communities to govern their educational practices?

2. In what ways have I advocated for policies that honor Native educational sovereignty?

3. Reflect on a recent initiative: How did it align with the principles of Native sovereignty?

Self-Evaluation Instrument:

- Rate your understanding of Native educational sovereignty from 1 to 5.

- Identify two specific actions you have taken to support Native educational sovereignty.

- Outline an area for improvement in embracing Native sovereignty and your plan to address it.

Chapter Three
Pillar Two: Decolonizing Leadership Practices

Diversity and Inclusion do not mean the same as decolonization. The former is about preserving this colonial reality & the latter is about dismantling it.

- Dr. Rosales Meza, source

Understanding Decolonization

Decolonization is a process aimed at unlearning and dismantling the structures and ideologies of colonialism to restore autonomy to Indigenous peoples. It seeks to address the injustices inflicted by British and European imperialism and to reinstate the sovereignty, identity, and rights of formerly colonized communities. This process is not uniform; it varies significantly depending on context and community and is multifaceted, encompassing social, cultural, economic, and psychological dimensions. It confronts the ongoing impacts of colonialism in our societies today. Decolonization can be daunting, particularly for those who have benefited from colonial systems or who perceive a threat to their safety from these changes, especially within educational settings and leadership.

Education plays a crucial role in the decolonization process. By teaching culturally relevant content, we empower Indigenous peoples to reclaim their stories and histories. This includes integrating Indigenous topics into curricula, recognizing Indigenous knowledge as valid and valuable, and creating environments where Indigenous students can excel academically while feeling culturally secure.

Such an approach not only benefits Indigenous students but also enriches all learners by fostering a greater understanding of First Nations languages, cultures, and histories. Decolonizing education challenges Eurocentric perspectives and prompts individuals to examine the effects of colonialism on contemporary life critically.

Considering the complex process of decolonization in education reveals that the path to creating equitable and inclusive learning environments is fraught with challenges that demand deep reflection and proactive strategies. While decolonization aims to dismantle colonial legacies, it also requires a critical analysis of the biases that shape our actions and policies. Implicit bias, in particular, presents a significant obstacle to achieving decolonization goals, often operating beneath our awareness and subtly influencing decisions. Implicit bias refers to the unconscious preferences or aversions individuals may hold toward specific ideas, objects, or groups. This concept underscores the intricacies of human behavior and decision-making, revealing how biases can manifest without our conscious realization.

Implicit Bias

Bias is a natural inclination for or against an idea, object, or group. Implicit bias refers to the ways individuals may act in biased manners without being aware of it. This concept is defined as a behavioral phenomenon that requires explanation rather than simply a characteristic individuals possess to justify their actions (Gawronski et al., 2022).

Implicit Bias in Education and Its Impact on Students

Leaders in predominantly Native schools face an uncomfortable truth: unless they actively dismantle colonial educational practices, they risk causing harm to Native students, even with good intentions.

The legacy of colonization continues to affect Native students through subtle yet powerful mechanisms of implicit bias.

These biases have concrete effects, including:

- Negative impacts on students' mental health and behavior

- Decreased academic achievement

- Disproportionate disciplinary actions

- Underrepresentation in advanced academic programs

- Suppression of Native identities and cultural expression

While educators do not enter the profession intending to harm, implicit biases operate unconsciously, creating school environments that can be unwelcoming or hostile to Native students' cultural identities and ways of knowing. This is particularly concerning because teachers and administrators responsible for ensuring educational equity work within a social system where racial biases are deeply ingrained and often unrecognized.

To foster truly equitable educational spaces, school leaders must:

- Actively identify and confront their own implicit biases

- Examine how colonial practices persist in their school systems

- Implement culturally responsive teaching methods

- Create environments that celebrate and sustain Native identities

- Engage in ongoing professional development focused on cultural competency

Achieving genuine educational equity requires more than just good intentions; it demands a conscious effort to recognize, understand, and actively counter the implicit biases that shape our educational institutions.

Implicit Bias and Leadership

School leaders play a crucial role in fostering a positive learning environment for all students. They need to identify and eliminate both explicit and implicit biases that can marginalize students, as these biases significantly impact various aspects of a student's educational experience.

Implicit bias can profoundly influence decision-making and interactions within educational settings, particularly affecting Native American students. non-Native school leaders may unintentionally allow their biases to shape their decisions, resulting in differential treatment of Native students. This often manifests as lower academic expectations, unequal resource distribution, and disciplinary inconsistencies. Data reveals significant disparities in discipline and academic performance expectations between Native and non-Native students, creating an environment where Native students face additional challenges and often feel marginalized and unsupported.

During the 2017–18 academic year, Native American students were suspended at a rate of 7%, exceeding the 5% average suspension rate for all other student groups. Historically, Native American students have faced higher suspension rates than their peers in both elementary and secondary schools, highlighting a persistent pattern of biased disciplinary practices (Leung-Gagné et al., 2022).

Implicit biases also influence curriculum and representation within schools. non-Native school leaders may unintentionally prioritize specific perspectives in educational materials, leading to the underrepresentation of Native American history and culture. This lack of representation can hinder Native students from seeing themselves reflected in their educational experiences, negatively impacting their sense of identity and belonging. Additionally, biased decision-making can affect speaker invitations and the content taught, reinforcing stereotypes and exclusion.

The effects of implicit bias extend to school policies and culture. Leadership biases can permeate the system, resulting in insufficient support for Native American students and a lack of culturally relevant practices. These biases can also influence hiring and promotion practices, limiting the representation of Native educators and leaders in the school district, thereby perpetuating a cycle of underrepresentation and inequity.

Disciplinary disparities further illustrate the impact of implicit bias. Retributive discipline raises concerns, as Native American students often face harsher penalties than their non-Native American counterparts for similar infractions. This inequity undermines their potential for success in an environment that should facilitate upward mobility. As long as these biases remain unaddressed, the cycle of disadvantage continues.

non-Native school leaders may remain unaware of their biases because these stereotypes are seldom confronted in conversations with those outside their racial background. Failing to address these issues allows biases to persist and influence school practices and policies. To create a more equitable environment for all students, training and awareness programs must be implemented to eliminate these biases. Schools and their leaders must take proactive steps to dismantle the barriers created by implicit bias and work towards long-term success for Native American students.

Decolonizing Leadership Practices

Decolonizing school leadership practices is a complex but essential effort to create more equitable, inclusive, and culturally responsive educational environments. By dismantling colonial structures and mindsets, school leaders can foster learning spaces that recognize diversity, address historical injustices, and prepare all students for life in a multicultural society.

Non-Native school leaders must actively work to decolonize the colonial legacies present in education, particularly at the K-12 level. This effort involves dismantling oppressive systems within schools and establishing practices that prioritize equity, justice, and cultural revitalization. School leaders should promote pedagogy that acknowledges and empowers Native cultures. The decolonization of leadership practices begins with recognizing that education often operates within colonial frameworks. Traditional colonial education models typically:

- Prioritize Western knowledge and epistemologies.

- Marginalize Indigenous and non-Western ways of knowing

- Maintain hierarchical power structures

- Encourage assimilation instead of cultural preservation

- Overlook the diverse needs and experiences of students from various cultural backgrounds

The Need for a Decolonized School Leadership Practice

Fostering Equity and Social Justice:

Decolonizing leadership aims to dismantle systemic racism that has historically disadvantaged Indigenous minority students by developing equitable practices. To ensure all students achieve similar levels of success, we must challenge the power structures rooted in colonialism.

Increasing Cultural Responsiveness:

Decolonial approaches encourage school leaders to recognize, honor, and integrate diverse cultural perspectives into educational policies, curricula, and practices. This cultural responsiveness enhances student engagement, academic performance, and overall well-being.

Promoting Inclusive Decision-Making:

Decolonizing leadership shifts away from traditional, authoritative decision-making towards collaborative, group-centered practices that respect and acknowledge multiple viewpoints.

Advancing Cultural Revitalization:

Cultural revitalization is essential. By challenging the dominance of Western worldviews, decolonial leadership creates space for Indigenous languages and ways of knowing.

Addressing Historical Trauma:

Decolonizing practices recognize and confront the historical trauma inflicted by colonial education systems. This approach fosters healing within communities by building trust between schools and their communities.

Advancing Diversity:

Decolonial education better equips all students to navigate and contribute to an interconnected globalized world.

Development of Critical Thinking:

Decolonial approaches expose students to diverse perspectives and alternative ways of knowing, enhancing their critical thinking skills and helping them understand the complexities of various issues.

Practical Steps for Decolonizing School Leadership Practices

School leaders must engage in self-reflection to recognize their biases and colonial mindsets. This process involves dismantling outdated thought patterns and adopting new perspectives.

- Implement collaborative decision-making mechanisms that include diverse voices, especially from historically marginalized communities. This may involve creating advisory boards or adopting consensus-based models.

- Decolonize the curriculum by integrating diverse perspectives and narratives.

- Critically examine Eurocentric historical narratives.

- Incorporate Indigenous Ways of Knowing.

- Promote the critical analysis of the impacts of colonialism.

- Provide ongoing cultural competence training for all staff to ensure they understand diverse cultures, identify biases, and apply culturally relevant practices.

- Foster authentic partnerships with local communities, particularly Indigenous and minority groups, by involving them in school governance, curriculum development, and cultural initiatives.

- Explore methods to preserve Indigenous languages and promote multilingual education to prevent their extinction.

- Review restorative justice techniques to eliminate punitive approaches that disproportionately affect marginalized students.

- Actively recruit and retain staff and leadership from diverse backgrounds, ensuring their racial and ethnic identities reflect those of the students in their district.

- Encourage and support teachers in implementing culturally responsive practices that acknowledge diverse learning styles and cultural backgrounds.

- Develop decolonial assessment practices that support non-standardized evaluations of knowledge and skills, moving beyond standardized tests that often perpetuate colonial biases.

Tools for Reflective Growth

Now that you have finished this chapter, take a moment to reflect on the following self-reflection questions, which are centered around the core pillar discussed here. These prompts aim to facilitate your personal and professional growth as a non-Native school leader. They will help you evaluate your practices and strengthen your commitment to Indigenous educational sovereignty, decolonizing leadership, prioritizing Indigenous knowledge, culturally affirming practices, and fostering authentic collaboration with Native communities.

Thoughtfully engaging with these questions will enhance your effectiveness as a respectful and inclusive advocate for Indigenous students and the communities you serve.

Self-Reflection Questions:

1. What steps have I taken to identify and challenge colonial mindsets in my leadership approach?

2. How do I integrate decolonization principles into my school's policies and practices?

3. Reflecting on my decision-making processes: Do they prioritize Indigenous perspectives and values?

Self-Evaluation Instrument:

- Rate your progress in decolonizing your leadership practices on a scale from 1 to 5.

- List three specific changes you have made to decolonize your leadership.

- Create a personal action plan for further decolonization efforts in the upcoming school year.

Chapter Four
Pillar Three: Prioritizing Indigenous Knowledge

If people can't acknowledge the wisdom of indigenous cultures, then that's their loss.

- Jay Griffiths, source

Indigenous Knowledge

Indigenous knowledge encompasses the diverse and evolving body of science, practices, and philosophies that Indigenous peoples have cultivated within their communities over generations. This knowledge is rooted in their relationships with the land, environment, and both human and non-human entities. It includes traditional practices, ecological understanding, oral histories, languages, and cultural values that are integral to Indigenous identities. Recognizing the significance of this knowledge is crucial not only for preserving and protecting these communities but also for providing learning opportunities that can expand our collective understanding. Indigenous knowledge affirms the unique perspectives and experiences of Indigenous peoples, fostering a sense of identity and belonging for many Indigenous students.

Acknowledging the depth of Indigenous knowledge related to environmental stewardship, biodiversity, and social justice is just the beginning. To genuinely prioritize Indigenous communities, we must actively listen to their voices, respect their sovereignty, and weave Indigenous knowledge systems into the core of educational philosophies, practices, and policies. This transformation calls for advocacy to amplify Indigenous voices, promote collaboration, and introduce new frameworks that recognize the vital role of Indigenous knowledge in creating a more equitable and just educational landscape.

As educational leaders, prioritizing Indigenous knowledge can have an immediate and profound impact on fostering an inclusive and equitable learning environment that honors the diverse cultural backgrounds of all students. Given their influence in shaping school vision, policies, and practices, educational leaders' commitment to integrating Indigenous knowledge will significantly enhance student engagement, achievement, and identity development.

Moving Beyond Curricular Inclusion to Leadership Integration

In education, integrating Indigenous knowledge systems presents both an opportunity and a significant challenge. The obstacles are multifaceted, including issues related to financing, entrenched colonial attitudes, funding constraints, inequalities in standardized testing, behavioral assessment frameworks, and curriculum design legislation. These challenges are further intensified by the shortage of Indigenous educators, resulting from historical and systemic forces that have marginalized Indigenous perspectives.

To create an educational environment that honors Indigenous epistemologies, school leaders must ensure that resources are allocated for Indigenous language instruction and culturally relevant materials. However, the colonial ideologies that underpin current practices continue to dominate educational assumptions, limiting our understanding of Indigenous knowledge. This influence extends to the sciences, where systemic racism and colonialism often lead to the devaluation or outright dismissal of Indigenous ways of knowing.

Fiscal constraints and restrictive financial criteria further hinder many Indigenous knowledge projects from achieving their goals. Additionally, standardized testing and curricular standards, which are rooted in Western educational models, offer little flexibility for alternative teaching approaches.

The lack of Indigenous educators in the academic workforce further complicates efforts to implement a culturally sensitive curriculum. Authentic engagement with Indigenous knowledge is most effective when delivered by educators who possess not only foundational understanding but also deep connections to Indigenous culture.

Addressing these challenges necessitates a strategic approach. This includes providing essential professional development for teachers to equip them with the knowledge and skills to teach Indigenous perspectives within anti-oppressive, justice-oriented frameworks. Collaboration with Indigenous communities is crucial, as such partnerships can facilitate knowledge sharing and resource development relevant to their cultural contexts.

Advocating for policy change is another critical strategy aimed at dismantling the colonial barriers that obstruct the decolonization of Indigenous knowledge in educational systems. Investing in resources developed through an Indigenous lens can make academic content more inclusive and help preserve and amplify Indigenous epistemologies.

Furthermore, promoting Indigenous leadership within educational systems will support the development of curricula grounded in Indigenous knowledge. This approach to emergent pedagogies allows educators to integrate Indigeneity into their practices, enriching students' learning experiences and fostering an inclusive environment that respects Indigenous knowledge.

In summary, incorporating Indigenous knowledge into education transcends academic considerations; it requires sustained, global efforts. By addressing these barriers, we can create a more inclusive educational model that values the diversity of Indigenous knowledge systems.

The Role of Indigenous Knowledge in Shaping Leadership Philosophy

Western pedagogical frameworks have mainly shaped the global educational landscape. However, there is a growing consensus on the need to integrate diverse epistemological perspectives, particularly Indigenous knowledge systems, into contemporary educational leadership. While Western frameworks have advanced education, they often overlook the rich insights found in Indigenous leadership and epistemologies. This scholarly effort advocates for incorporating Indigenous intellectual traditions into educational leadership practices, moving beyond mere academic diversity to embrace a holistic worldview rooted in balance and life-affirming principles.

To authentically prioritize Indigenous knowledge in educational leadership, a significant shift is required from tokenistic inclusion to a comprehensive integration of Indigenous philosophical principles.

Prioritizing Indigenous knowledge is not just about inclusion; it represents a transformative imperative that embraces the values of balance, harmony, and respect found in many Indigenous cultures. By learning from Indigenous leaders, educational systems can foster environments that unify mind, body, and spirit in the pursuit of knowledge. This transformation demands ongoing dialogue, collaboration, and a commitment to challenge and reshape Western educational paradigms, thereby recognizing and leveraging the full potential of Indigenous knowledge to navigate the complexities of the modern world.

Case Study:

Indigenous Perspective on Leadership

Introduction

This case study, authored by Epenesa Esera (2023), a member of the Faculty of Education at the National University of Samoa and published in the Sociology International Journal, explores the incorporation of the Samoan leadership model into the education system. This model is founded on *alofa* (love) and is characterized by collective and servant leadership frameworks. It emphasizes the integration of Indigenous values with Western leadership concepts, focusing on community and shared responsibilities. This approach is particularly impactful in educational settings, enhancing the relevance of teaching and learning practices.

Fundamental Samoan-Style Leadership Components

Alofa and Servant Leadership

- Alofa, a core principle of the Samoan leadership model, represents love, care, and service to others, distinct from romantic interpretations.

- The model prioritizes the well-being of the group over individual interests. Decisions are made by consensus, typically requiring over 75% agreement, and conflict is discouraged.

- *Matai*, or leaders, are chosen for their ability to serve rather than for personal prestige, with a focus on the best interests of their family or village.

Synthesis with Western Notions

The Samoan leadership model effectively merges Indigenous values with Western leadership practices, creating a culturally authentic and practical approach with global relevance. This synthesis signifies a shift toward transcultural leadership practices that educate humanity through a cross-cultural lens.

Application in Education

Examples of Servant Leadership in Educational Settings

- At the Faculty of Education at the National University of Samoa, research investigates the conceptualization and application of essential pedagogical servant leadership attributes.

- Key topics include best practices, presentation skills, mentoring techniques, team-building and collaboration strategies, and empowerment methods.

- This teaching approach cultivates an atmosphere of listening, empathy, healing, awareness, and influence, promoting personal and community growth.

Cultural and Social Impact

The Samoan leadership model reflects the culture and showcases various leadership styles and peaceful coexistence. It represents a service-oriented educational initiative that emphasizes community welfare and fosters an environment where individuals can rise above societal prejudices and divisions.

Conclusion

By building on the Indigenous principle of alofa, the Samoan leadership model adeptly integrates Western and Indigenous practices. It highlights community, service, and shared responsibility, infusing culturally relevant leadership styles into challenging environments. This model not only preserves a strong Samoan cultural identity but also enhances educational outcomes by fostering an inclusive and supportive atmosphere where everyone feels a sense of belonging.

Tools for Reflective Growth

Now that you have finished this chapter, take some time to reflect on the following self-reflection questions, which are centered around the core themes discussed here. These prompts are intended to support your personal and professional growth as a non-Native school leader. They will help you evaluate your practices and strengthen your commitment to Indigenous educational sovereignty, decolonizing leadership, prioritizing Indigenous knowledge, culturally affirming practices, and fostering authentic collaboration with Native communities.

Thoughtfully engaging with these questions will enhance your effectiveness as a respectful and inclusive advocate for Indigenous students and the communities you serve.

Self-Reflection Questions:

1. How do I actively incorporate Indigenous knowledge and perspectives into my leadership decisions?

2. In what ways have I promoted the integration of Indigenous cultural content into the curriculum?

3. Reflecting on my professional development, have I sought out learning opportunities that focus on Indigenous knowledge?

Self-Evaluation Instrument:

- Rate your prioritization of Indigenous knowledge in your leadership on a scale from 1 to 5.

- Provide three examples of how Indigenous knowledge has shaped your leadership practices.

- Develop a strategy to improve the integration of Indigenous knowledge in your school.

Chapter Five

Pillar Four: Using Culturally Affirming Leadership Practices

Indigenous people have long been telling the world that our knowledge, culture, and way of life are essential not just to us but to the rest of the world.

Wilma Mankiller, source

Defining Culturally Affirming Practices

As educational environments become increasingly diverse, leaders must embrace culturally affirming leadership practices to create genuinely inclusive spaces. While culturally relevant and responsive practices are essential for connecting students' cultural backgrounds to their learning, culturally affirming practices go a step further. These practices celebrate and integrate individual cultural identities into a cohesive community, recognizing these multiple identities as valuable contributions that enhance societal productivity.

By prioritizing culturally affirming practices, leaders ensure that all community members feel recognized, appreciated, and empowered, enriching the educational experience for everyone involved. This commitment requires leaders to ensure that the curriculum reflects the histories, cultures, and perspectives of Native peoples. This includes incorporating Native languages, traditions, and knowledge systems into the classroom while actively challenging stereotypes and biases that perpetuate colonial narratives.

Differences Between Culturally Affirming, Relevant, and Responsive Practices

In today's evolving educational landscape, honoring and affirming the unique cultural identities of all students is more critical than ever. As our schools become more culturally diverse, academic leaders must foster environments that not only tolerate but fully embrace the rich tapestry of students' lifestyles. The discourse on educational equity has often centered around "culturally responsive" and "culturally relevant" practices, which have guided efforts to meet the needs of all learners. However, these approaches can make broad generalizations about student identities, potentially overlooking the unique facets of Native students in predominantly Native schools.

This chapter aims to clarify the distinctions between culturally responsive and relevant practices, highlighting their limitations in serving Native communities. We advocate for the normalization of culturally affirming practices—a perspective that goes beyond mere responsiveness or relevance to actively celebrate and validate Native identities and cultures.

Over the past decade, culturally responsive and relevant pedagogy has been recognized as crucial for supporting diverse student populations. These concepts have shaped learning environments that honor and include cultural practices, regardless of students' cultural heritage. However, as education evolves, our understanding must progress beyond mere responsiveness and relevance toward deeper engagement through culturally affirming practices.

This shift is significant in schools with substantial populations of Native students, where all school leaders, especially non-Native ones, should prioritize validating and honoring their students' identities and cultures.

We aim to illuminate the unique role of culturally affirming education in empowering Native students and fostering an environment where their cultural heritage is recognized and celebrated. This involves transforming leadership to create space for Native identities and encouraging open dialogues about the true history of this land, whether regarding First Nations or European influences. We call upon every educational leader to rise to this challenge and engage in honest dialogue to set a new standard of inclusivity and respect that can serve as a model for schools everywhere.

The chapter will explore the critical necessity and transformative potential of shifting toward cultural affirmation within our educational institutions. We argue that acknowledging Native identities and cultures should be foundational, an integral part of our schools that informs every aspect of teaching. This approach leads to a more equitable, inclusive, and culturally rich educational system in which students are recognized and appreciated for who they truly are.

Culturally Relevant Pedagogy

Culturally relevant pedagogy is an educational approach that incorporates students' cultural backgrounds into the teaching and learning process. Analyzing the term reveals its key components and overall significance.

- Culturally: This refers to the customs, beliefs, values, practices, and social behaviors of specific groups or societies that shape their identities and experiences.

- Relevant: This term indicates the importance of connecting educational content and methods to students' cultural experiences and realities.

- Pedagogy: This encompasses the art, science, and practice of teaching, including the methods educators use to facilitate learning.

By integrating these elements, culturally relevant pedagogy emerges as an approach that makes teaching meaningful and applicable to students' cultural contexts. It operates on the premise that students learn best when educational content relates to their lives and experiences.

The emphasis is on the central role of culture in pedagogy, suggesting that culture should not be a peripheral consideration but a fundamental component that informs curriculum design, instructional strategies, and classroom interactions.

Critical aspects of culturally relevant pedagogy include:

- Academic Success: Connecting new knowledge to students' cultural backgrounds enhances comprehension and retention, facilitating mastery of subject matter.

- Cultural Competence: Encouraging students to value their own cultures while gaining fluency in at least one other culture fosters a deeper understanding of themselves and others.

- Critical Consciousness: Developing students' ability to analyze social injustices and inequities critically empowers them to become agents of change within their communities.

A semantic analysis of the term highlights its commitment to:

- Inclusiveness: Celebrating the rich cultural capital that every student brings to school.

- Engagement: Increasing student attendance by reflecting their cultural experiences in learning.

- Empowerment: Affirming students' cultural perspectives to support academic mastery and social-emotional success.

In summary, culturally relevant pedagogy emphasizes integrating culture into education to enhance student engagement, critical thinking, and academic success. These pedagogical practices connect students to their stories, with education serving as a tool for unity and change.

Culturally Responsive Pedagogy

What is culturally responsive pedagogy? Culturally responsive pedagogy is a teaching philosophy that acknowledges the integral role of a student's cultural background in the learning process. Incorporating this understanding into education enhances the relevance and applicability of knowledge. Educators across the country aim for inclusivity, and this approach highlights the advantages of affirming students' cultural identities, fostering an inclusive learning environment that supports both academic success and social-emotional development.

To grasp the concept of culturally responsive pedagogy, we can break it down into its key components.

Cultural

- Cultural Recognition: This aspect acknowledges that culture shapes a student's identity and influences their perceptions and interactions with the world. Culture encompasses the customs, beliefs, values, and social norms that students internalize from their families and communities.

- Interpretive Frameworks: Students' cultural backgrounds serve as lenses through which they comprehend and engage with academic content. Educators must understand these cultural frameworks to provide instruction that resonates with students.

Responsive

- Responsive Teaching: This refers to an educator's ability to perceive and appropriately address the diverse cultural and sociolinguistic needs present in their classroom. Effective teaching acknowledges and appeals to the rich tapestry of cultural backgrounds represented.

- Empathetic Engagement: This aspect of responsiveness reflects an educator's empathy and commitment to fostering an inclusive learning environment that values cultural differences.

Pedagogy

- Pedagogy: The art and science of teaching encompasses curriculum design, instructional methods, and assessments, ultimately shaping the teaching approach.

- Educational Theory and Practice: This involves understanding how students learn best and identifying effective practices to enhance learning.

Essential Qualities of Culturally Responsive *Pedagogy*

Culturally responsive pedagogy is characterized by several interrelated features that contribute to a holistic educational approach.

Asset-Based Perspective

- Recognizing Cultural Diversity: Educators view cultural differences as opportunities to enrich learning rather than challenges to be resolved. This perspective allows for the incorporation of diverse cultural experiences, enhancing the educational experience.

- Using Cultural Capital: Teachers can connect students to relevant and meaningful learning experiences by leveraging the cultural capital students bring.

Relational Teaching

- Authentic Relationships: Establishing and nurturing quality relationships between teachers and students is fundamental to this pedagogical approach. Through these interpersonal connections, teachers show genuine interest in students' lives and foster open communication.

- Appreciation of Culture: Educators demonstrate respect for students' cultural heritages, which can enhance relationships within the classroom.

Cultural Competence

Learning About Cultures: Culturally aware teachers engage deeply with their students' cultural contexts, continuously learning about various artistic practices, beliefs, and communication styles.

Culturally Infused Instruction: Educators use this cultural knowledge to shape their teaching methods, ensuring that instruction is culturally responsive and relevant for all students.

Critical Consciousness

- Cultivating Critical Analysis: Students are encouraged to develop a critical consciousness that helps them identify and challenge social injustices and inadequacies.

- Socially Relevant Curriculum: The curriculum is designed to involve students in community-based social issues, fostering socially aware and committed individuals.

Aligned to Curriculum and Content

- Inclusive Curriculum Design: The curriculum intentionally includes a diverse range of cultures, perspectives, and experiences, helping students understand that their identities are valued within the educational system.

- Diverse Literature: Incorporating texts and examples from various cultures makes the curriculum more relatable and provides opportunities for students to explore new ideas.

Learning Community

- Fostering an Inclusive Environment: Classrooms are structured to value diversity and implement practices that ensure all members feel included.

- Mutual Respect and Collaboration: Students are encouraged to share their cultural experiences, promoting empathy and respect for others' backgrounds.

Enhanced Learning Outcomes

- Heightened Engagement: Educational materials that resonate with students' cultural experiences enhance their engagement and motivation, leading to improved comprehension and retention.

- Improved Academic Performance: Research consistently shows that culturally responsive instruction is linked to better academic outcomes for students from diverse backgrounds.

Building Positive Cultural Identity Development

- Building Self-Confidence: When educators affirm cultural diversity, students gain greater self-confidence.

- Empowering Students: This teaching approach equips students with a sense of agency that is often lacking in their communities.

Promotion of Social Cohesion

- Respect for Others: Culturally responsive pedagogy fosters understanding among different cultural groups, creating an atmosphere of cooperation and community spirit.

- Preparation for a Diverse Society: Students learn to navigate a multicultural environment with responsibility, respect, and success.

Teaching through culturally responsive pedagogy is an ongoing journey that demands reflection and growth from educators. It represents a commitment to embracing students' cultural realities and transforming instructional practices. This approach positions education as a vital force for universal understanding, where diversity is seen as an opportunity for growth through perseverance and mutual respect.

Culturally affirming leadership is a targeted approach to educational leadership that values and celebrates the cultural diversity within a school community. It goes beyond mere acknowledgment; it integrates the cultural experiences of students, teachers, and staff at every level of the school.

Components of a Culturally Affirming Leader

- Cultural Recognition: Leaders acknowledge and validate the diverse cultural identities within their school community.

- Cultural Advocacy: They ensure that all cultural groups can advocate for their needs equally.

- Cultural Integration: Leaders incorporate cultural perspectives and practices into school policies, curricula, and activities.

Culturally responsive teaching and culturally relevant pedagogy focus on enhancing interactions between teachers and students in the classroom and on honoring and integrating students' cultural backgrounds into learning. In contrast, culturally affirming leadership operates at the school or system level, shaping policies and environments that support cultural diversity. Together, these approaches address different levels within education, each emphasizing unique yet complementary aspects of helping students from diverse backgrounds.

Culturally responsive pedagogy is rooted in classroom instruction, making teachers more attuned to each student's history and lived experiences. This responsiveness fosters predictable services and instructional methods that stimulate learning in line with cultural traditions.

Strategies in culturally responsive pedagogy include modeling instruction based on students' cultural experiences, using real-life and contextually relevant examples, and connecting classroom learning to students' cultural backgrounds and knowledge.

In contrast, culturally relevant pedagogy, grounded in educational theory and practice, promotes academic success, cultural competence, and social change through critical consciousness, operating at a different level than leadership.

Culturally affirming leadership, on the other hand, functions at the organizational level, influencing school-wide policies and practices. Leaders who engage in culturally affirming actions affect the educational landscape, impacting students, teachers, staff, and parents. They develop strategic plans that prioritize cultural affirmation in the mission, professional development, resource allocation, and community partnerships. These leaders strive to create a school culture where individuals can express their identities freely and confidently, ensuring that all students feel included, regardless of their backgrounds. Key actions in culturally affirming leadership promote inclusion and equity by regularly reviewing policies to foster a non-discriminatory, inclusive environment and ensuring access to resources and opportunities for all students, teachers, and staff.

When effectively implemented, culturally affirming leadership can yield numerous positive outcomes. It can enhance student achievement; students who feel recognized and valued by their teachers and school leaders tend to perform better academically and maintain higher self-esteem. They are often more motivated and engaged in their learning. Furthermore, it can boost morale and improve school culture. When educators and support staff feel integral to the learning community, they foster an atmosphere of respect and welcome. Celebrating diversity directly reduces prejudice and encourages respect and collaboration among all members of the school community.

Culturally affirming leadership is intrinsically linked to an active approach to educational leadership that embeds culturally relevant practices throughout the school. It requires school leaders to integrate diversity into the school's daily operations intentionally. By doing so, leaders ensure that everyone in the school community feels safe, supported, and empowered to thrive.

Implementing Affirming Practices in Leadership

- Articulate and Promote Inclusive Values: Leaders must clearly express and demonstrate values that celebrate cultural diversity rather than suppress it within their organizations. This involves establishing a framework that acknowledges the significance of cultural identities and integrates them prominently into the community's core values.

- Leaders should regularly review their policies to ensure they promote cultural affirmation and remain relevant. This requires evaluating laws and procedures in ways that reflect the diverse cultural backgrounds present in the school community.

- Encourage Affirming Spaces: Leaders should model and cultivate environments where cultural identities are recognized, acknowledged, and celebrated. This includes implementing processes, behaviors, and policies that support students' and staff's understanding of their cultural backgrounds.

- Identify and Use Strengths: Leaders should exemplify asset-based approaches by recognizing and building upon the strengths, diversity, and culture of colleagues and students. This perspective views cultural diversity as a valuable resource rather than a challenge to be addressed.

- Hiring Practices: Culturally affirming leadership entails hiring staff who share lived experiences with the students they serve, fostering empathy and relatability among all community members.

- Empower Educators: Leaders should empower educators, particularly those from underrepresented backgrounds, by granting them the autonomy to adapt instructional practices in culturally relevant and empowering ways. This enables educators to tailor their approaches to meet the needs of an increasingly diverse student population.

Tools for Reflective Growth

As you conclude this chapter, take time to reflect on the following self-reflection questions, which are structured around the core concepts discussed. These prompts are designed to facilitate your personal and professional growth as a non-Native school leader, helping you evaluate your practices and strengthen your commitment to Indigenous educational sovereignty, decolonizing leadership, prioritizing Indigenous knowledge, culturally affirming practices, and authentic collaboration with Native communities.

Engaging thoughtfully with these questions will enhance your effectiveness as an advocate for Indigenous students and the communities you serve.

Self-Reflection Questions:

1. How do I create a school environment that affirms and celebrates Indigenous cultures?

2. In what ways have I involved Indigenous students and families in shaping school culture and practices?

3. Reflecting on my approach to discipline and behavior management: How does it align with culturally affirming practices?

Self-Evaluation Instrument:

- Rate your culturally affirming practices on a scale from 1 to 5.

- List three initiatives you have implemented that affirm Indigenous culture within the school.

- Identify one area for improvement in culturally affirming practices and outline your plan to address it.

Chapter Six

Pillar Five: Purposeful Collaboration with Indigenous Communities

They come to understand that a motivated, connected tribe engaged in a movement holds far greater power than a larger group ever could. Generous and authentic leadership will consistently triumph over the self-serving actions of someone who participates merely out of a sense of capability (Godin, 2008).

At its core, tribal consultation is a form of communication. It establishes the legal framework that allows tribes and the federal government to discuss anticipated decisions. This communication is crucial not just for its own sake but also because it directly influences the decision-making process. However, decision-makers may view tribal consultations as merely another procedural hurdle in the bureaucratic system. This perspective can create a gap in expectations regarding what constitutes a successful consultation for each party involved.

For tribes, success often means that the ideas or outcomes they advocate for are adopted, either fully or partially. In Navajo tradition, success may also be defined by achieving unexpected solutions through open dialogue and consensus-building. Conversely, federal agencies might define success by adherence to procedural correctness—such as adequately consulting with tribes—even if the consultation is superficial and the tribes' input is not genuinely taken into account. This divergence in defining success can complicate the consultation process.

The Importance of Collaboration in Educational Leadership

Facilitating meaningful and authentic collaboration should be a primary goal for non-Native school leaders working in predominantly Native schools. In these unique educational contexts, collaborative efforts become more impactful when they foster decision-making partnerships that honor Native educational sovereignty. Through intentional collaboration, non-Native school leaders demonstrate their commitment to understanding the cultural, historical, and educational rights of Native peoples.

In primarily Native school communities, collaboration extends beyond mere cooperation; it seeks to establish inclusive decision-making partnerships that respect the cultural and educational sovereignty of Native stakeholders. By engaging with Native community members, non-Native leaders acknowledge their expertise in shaping a vision for the education of Native children. Meaningful collaboration reflects respect for Native educational systems. It signifies a willingness to listen, learn, and make decisions aligned with the values, traditions, and long-term goals of the Native community.

Leaders recognize that Native communities have the fundamental right to determine how their children are educated, ensuring that their culture, traditions, and knowledge are honored. This necessitates shared decision-making through inclusive partnerships.

By involving Native community members, leaders ensure that the specific needs, perspectives, and aspirations of Native students and families are prioritized in educational planning and policy decisions, leading to more culturally responsive outcomes. Collaborating with Native community members allows leaders to deepen their understanding of cultural traditions and kinship practices, which is essential for guiding the development of educational programs curricular enhancements, and other culturally relevant initiatives.

Collaborative decision-making addresses the academic, social, emotional, and cultural needs of all Native students. Through this collaboration, leaders can develop targeted interventions, support systems, and enrichment opportunities that promote positive educational outcomes for Native students.

Collaboration creates a space for Native voices to be heard and valued, ensuring that parents, grandparents, and students have a seat at the decision-making table. Each school and district has the autonomy to implement laws effectively. When leaders actively engage Native stakeholders—listening as much as they speak—they demonstrate their commitment to honoring Native knowledge, perspectives, and experiences within educational frameworks.

This collaborative approach empowers Native communities to exercise self-determination in decisions affecting their children's education. Tribes can establish educational aspirations, create meaningful and relevant curricula, and allocate resources that best serve their students. Such collaboration fosters the protection and sharing of Indigenous culture within schools. Together, leaders and Native community members can develop cultural programs, language classes, and cultural competency training for staff to help Native students maintain a sense of cultural pride.

Effective collaboration is built on trust and strong relationships. For non-native school leaders, it is crucial to cultivate relationships with Native community members and to express a genuine interest in their perspectives and needs. Regular and meaningful community engagement—through meetings, cultural activities, and one-on-one conversations—will foster the necessary respect and understanding.

Implementing frameworks that promote shared decision-making, such as advisory committees and community councils, provides Native voices with a formal role in the decision-making process. These structures enable ongoing communication, collective decision-making, and collaborative problem-solving, ensuring that the Native community's priorities and concerns are acknowledged and addressed.

School leaders of non-Native heritage must continually develop their cultural engagement skills and embrace cultural humility. Embracing cultural humility involves learning about the history, customs, and current realities of Native communities. By recognizing their own limitations and biases, leaders can foster collaboration and learning, paving the way for an inclusive decision-making process.

Building trust within Native school communities and navigating the complexities of collaboration requires an understanding of power dynamics and historical trauma. non-Native leaders should acknowledge their positional power and actively work to redistribute it through collaborative practices. Establishing trust and collaboration that is trauma-informed and healing-centered necessitates a commitment to addressing historical trauma.

It is crucial to avoid tokenism or superficial inclusion. Collaboration must go beyond performative gestures or the involvement of a few individuals; it should engage authentically with various aspects of Native community life. Leaders must be intentional in their efforts and refrain from replicating colonial practices of exclusion. Tokenistic approaches that marginalize Native voices do not constitute true collaboration; they perpetuate past injustices and must be avoided.

In predominantly Native school communities, collaboration is essential to effective leadership. Successful non-Native school leaders honor Native educational sovereignty through their partnerships. By elevating Native voices, collaboration allows the education of Native youth to be shaped by the experiences, insights, and aspirations of their communities. Through collective decision-making partnerships, leaders can promote academic success, preserve culture, and ensure the well-being of Native students.

Meaningful Collaboration as Mandated by Law

Effective leadership in predominantly Native schools relies on collaboration with Native tribes. This collaboration is not only a best practice but also a legal obligation. Title I funds, which account for approximately 68% of all federally funded public schools, totaling nearly $14 billion, must be partnered with Native tribes meaningfully. Executive Order 13175 requires federal agencies to consult with tribal nations.

Tribal consultation is a formal, two-way, government-to-government process between federal agencies and tribal nations. It is essential for ensuring that the federal government meets its trust responsibilities and respects the sovereignty of tribal nations. This executive order mandates that federal agencies engage in meaningful consultation and collaboration with tribal governments when developing policies or programs that may impact them, covering areas such as education, health, and natural resources.

Thus, tribal consultation is critical for federal agencies and programs, including those managing education funding, to ensure that their decisions and actions align with the unique needs, priorities, and self-determination of Native communities.

Key elements of tribal consultation include:

- Timely Notice: Federal agencies must provide early and adequate notification to tribal nations regarding any proposed actions or policies that may affect them.

- Meaningful Dialogue: There must be authentic, two-way communication between federal officials and tribal representatives to gather input and feedback.

- Incorporation of Tribal Feedback: Federal agencies must clearly demonstrate how they have integrated the concerns and recommendations of tribal nations into their final decisions and implementation plans.

- Respect for Tribal Sovereignty: The consultation process must honor the inherent sovereignty of tribal nations and their right to self-determination, especially concerning the education of their children.

Federal agencies need to articulate how they have incorporated the feedback and concerns of tribal nations into their decision-making processes. This ensures that tribal input is not only acknowledged but also acted upon, thereby strengthening the tribal consultation process.

By adhering to these principles, school leaders can significantly align federal education funds, such as Title I, with the needs, priorities, and self-determination of Native communities. Their leadership in this collaborative approach can lead to more equitable and culturally responsive educational outcomes for Native students.

Importance of Formalizing Collaboration with Native Tribes Through MOAs and MOUs Strategies for Increasing Indigenous Voice in

Decision-Making

Redesigning collaboration with stakeholders in predominantly Native communities requires intentionality and a commitment to shared decision-making. While leaders often seek stakeholder input through parent-teacher conferences, climate surveys, and strategic planning, these approaches tend to solicit feedback after initiatives or decisions are already established. Authentic collaboration involves building together and seeking input on both the objectives and the methods of proposed initiatives, which necessitates humility from school leaders.

Approaching collaboration with humility and a focus on joint decision-making demonstrates a leader's commitment to sustaining Native educational sovereignty—the ability of Indigenous communities to govern and control their children's education.

Engaging authentically with Native stakeholders signals that school leaders value and respect the community's expertise, values, and priorities, and acknowledge its right to influence its children's education. This collaborative approach starkly contrasts with the historical and ongoing legacy of educational policies that have often marginalized Native voices and self-determination. When school leaders embrace collaboration with humility, they create space for Native stakeholders to actively participate in shaping educational experiences and outcomes for their children, allowing the community to assert its sovereignty over educational decisions.

Moreover, shifting from a paternalistic to a partnership-based relationship rooted in humility can help alleviate power imbalances. This transformation in the historical relationship between schools and Native communities offers hope for a more equitable and inclusive educational system, fostering optimism and anticipation.

Ultimately, this collaborative strategy embodies a leader's commitment to Native educational sovereignty. It reflects a deep trust in the community and a willingness to relinquish control, share power, and work authentically with community members to create educational experiences that address their unique needs, values, and aspirations.

Authentic collaboration with Native communities that honors their educational sovereignty requires a multidimensional approach.

Here are some strategies school leaders can implement:

- Cultivate Relationships and Build Trust: True collaboration begins with fostering genuine, lasting relationships with Native stakeholders. This involves active listening, learning about the community's history, values, and priorities, and demonstrating a genuine willingness to partner with the community.

- Welcome Shared Decision-Making: School leaders should establish structures for shared decision-making so that Native stakeholders are co-decision-makers rather than merely recipients of top-down initiatives. This can include collaboratively setting the vision, goals, and implementation plans for educational programs and policies.

- Adapt and Be Flexible: Collaborating with Native communities requires flexibility in adjusting timelines, communication styles, and even project scopes to align with community decision-making processes. School leaders should be open to adapting to the community's preferences.

- Be Transparent and Accountable: Maintain openness and transparency throughout the collaborative process. Provide regular updates, take responsibility for decisions, and create feedback loops to ensure community input is meaningfully integrated.

- Acknowledge and Honor Sovereignty: True collaboration must respect the sovereignty of Native communities over their children's education, deferring to their self-determination and resisting paternalistic or assimilationist approaches.

- Support Capacity Building: Invest in Native communities' capacity to engage fully in collaborative processes by providing resources, training, and technical assistance as needed. This investment empowers stakeholders and ensures that those wishing to participate meaningfully have the necessary tools.

Collectively, these strategies will help school leaders cultivate a collaborative culture that respects Native educational sovereignty, builds trust, and develops responsive educational experiences that reflect the community's needs and aspirations.

Examples of Successful Collaborative Initiatives

Collaboration that respects and honors Native educational sovereignty can be challenging, yet numerous examples illustrate how school leaders and Native communities have successfully worked together to create impactful educational experiences. These stories emphasize the importance of humility, shared decision-making, and a genuine commitment to self-determination.

These examples serve as valuable lessons, offering insights into the principles, strategies, and outcomes of school-Native partnerships. By examining these real-world instances, educational leaders can develop a practical blueprint for building authentic partnerships and safeguarding the educational sovereignty of Native communities. This knowledge empowers them to navigate the complexities of collaboration with confidence and understanding.

The following section presents several case studies that demonstrate the significant role that authentic collaboration can play in shaping educational programming. These studies showcase how school leaders and Native communities have partnered to create meaningful, empowering, and culturally relevant opportunities that reflect the community's values and aspirations. They illustrate the possibilities that arise from approaching collaboration with humility, flexibility, and a deep recognition of Native educational sovereignty.

Washington State

The Washington State Native American Education Advisory Committee (WSNAEAC) is a key organization established to guide and enhance the education of Native Americans in Washington. Reestablished in March 2019, it aims to support the academic success and cultural sovereignty of American Indian and Alaska Native (AIAN) students, aligning with the needs of the community, schools, and tribes. The 22-member committee, appointed by tribes and organizations, brings diverse tribal, urban, and educational perspectives to inform its work.

WSNAEAC is a strong advocate for collaboration, working closely with the Office of Superintendent of Public Instruction, the Office of Native Education, and the Washington State School Directors' Association. Together, they establish and refine tribal consultation processes that comply with federal law and enhance the educational experiences and outcomes for AIAN students. The committee also seeks to strengthen government-to-government relationships by reinstating regional meetings and allowing tribal councils and school district boards to discuss strategies to close the achievement gap for AIAN students.

One of WSNAEAC's key initiatives is the implementation of the Since Time Immemorial curriculum, which teaches students about tribal sovereignty, Native history, and perspectives within state learning standards. Despite some challenges, such as disagreements over the inclusion of federally recognized tribes in discussions, WSNAEAC remains focused on federal recognition and government-to-government relations to meet the educational needs of AIAN students.

WSNAEAC is committed to transparency and accountability, providing public access to committee minutes and bylaws while holding regular meetings to address ongoing and emerging issues. This commitment demonstrates the committee's dedication to keeping stakeholders informed and engaged.

In summary, WSNAEAC is a vital component of culturally relevant schooling and Native partnerships with schools in Washington State, making it essential for advancing Native education and recognizing Native sovereignty.

Minnesota

Minnesota has made significant progress in formalizing and enhancing the consultation process between the state government and tribal nations. Executive Order 13-10, signed by Governor Mark Dayton on April 12, 2013, mandates that all state agencies develop tribal consultation policies and engage in meaningful, government-to-government discussions with tribal nations regarding policies, programs, or decisions that may impact Native communities. In 2021, this order was codified into state law, solidifying the state's commitment to tribal consultation.

The tribal consultation process in Minnesota emphasizes early and ongoing engagement, meaningful incorporation of tribal input, and a dedication to addressing the unique needs and priorities of Native communities. State agencies are required to appoint tribal liaisons to facilitate this process and ensure that tribal voices are included in decision-making.

Minnesota's approach to tribal consultation is grounded in collaboration, aiming to build strong and respectful relationships between the state and tribal nations. This approach reflects a deep respect for the sovereign status of tribes and their inherent right to self-govern, particularly in matters related to the health and education of their children.

Through this commitment to collaboration, Minnesota is determined to uphold its trust obligations and support the educational, economic, and social well-being of tribal communities within the state.

New Mexico

New Mexico has enacted the State-Tribal Collaboration Act (STCA), a significant piece of legislation aimed at fostering partnerships between the state and Native American tribes. This bill was introduced to enhance relationships between governments and improve communication between state agencies and tribal governments. The STCA represents a comprehensive approach to promoting collaboration and dialogue between the state and tribes. It establishes a framework for government-to-government relations, cultural competence, and accountability to Native American communities, guiding state policies and programs related to the health and welfare of Native Americans and the administration of Native American affairs.

The collaboration framework formalizes a process for developing effective programs and services that directly benefit Native American citizens in New Mexico. It mandates that state agencies implement policies that encourage cooperation with sovereign tribal governments to ensure mutual benefits. Key components of the STCA are designed to achieve meaningful collaboration. Each cabinet-level agency is required to appoint a tribal liaison, train employees who work with tribes in cultural competency, and submit an annual report detailing the agency's achievements and ongoing efforts to strengthen government-to-government relations. This ensures that state agencies have the necessary information to engage appropriately with tribal entities.

Additional elements include:

- Cultural and Government Interactions: The STCA is based on the principle that effective governance is best achieved through culturally competent practices. Positive government-

92

to-government relations depend on the successful integration of diverse cultures and the formulation of policies that facilitate meaningful engagement while respecting the sovereignty and self-determination of Indigenous nations.

- Annual Summit and Reporting: The STCA establishes an annual State-Tribal Leaders Summit at which the governor meets with tribal leaders to discuss issues of mutual concern. It also requires a yearly report on state agency activities under the STCA to promote transparency and accountability.

- Definitions and Recognition: The STCA acknowledges the unique and essential role of Native American tribes in New Mexico and provides definitions for terms such as "American Indian or Alaska Native" and "Indian nation, tribe, or pueblo." These definitions align with New Mexico law and specifically include federally recognized entities within the state.

The STCA has significantly transformed state-tribal relations in New Mexico, creating institutional mechanisms for a more collaborative and consultative relationship. This has resulted in increased sensitivity to tribal interests and needs, leading to policies and programs that reflect a partnership mentality between the state and Native populations.

Tools for Reflective Growth

Now that you have finished this chapter, take time to consider the following self-reflection questions. These prompts are designed to guide your personal and professional growth as a non-Native school leader, helping you assess your practices and deepen your commitment to Indigenous educational sovereignty, decolonizing leadership, prioritizing Indigenous knowledge, culturally affirming practices, and authentic collaboration with Native communities.

Engaging thoughtfully with these questions will support you in becoming a more effective, respectful,

Self-Reflection Questions:

1. How can I build authentic partnerships with Native families, community leaders, and organizations?

2. In what ways have I actively engaged Native stakeholders in the school decision-making process?

3. Reflect on a recent collaborative project: How did it align with the values and needs of the Native community?

Self-Evaluation Instrument:

- Rate your effectiveness in collaborating with Native stakeholders on a scale of 1 to 5.

- Identify three partnerships you have established with Native community members or organizations.

- Outline a plan to strengthen authentic collaboration in the upcoming school year.

Chapter Seven

A Call to Action for non-Native Leaders

School leaders in predominantly Native communities are called to lead in ways that are uniquely responsive to the cultural influences shaping their students' lives and the communities they inhabit. Working in these environments requires thoughtful and respectful engagement with the cultural nuances and historical challenges faced by Native students. More than merely an administrative role, a non-Native school leader's position in these contexts is transformative, demanding a commitment to understanding, advocacy, and decisive action.

The urgency of this call to action cannot be overstated: non-Native leaders must approach their roles with cultural awareness, sensitivity, and active engagement. They should immerse themselves in local Native history, listen to Native students and educators, and advocate for the creation of educational spaces in which Native cultures are valued and integrated into the learning experience.

The need for action is increasingly pressing, as the prospects of Native students significantly impact their lives and the well-being of their tribes. Non-Native leaders have a responsibility to ensure that these students not only achieve academic success but also experience a profound sense of belonging rooted in their cultural identity within the school environment.

This moment demands that non-Native school leaders step up with commitment and courage. It is time to advocate for educational practices that affirm and sustain Native identities, decolonize contemporary educational systems, and foster genuine partnerships with Native nations and communities. These educational spaces should become beacons of cultural pride and academic achievement. This requires adopting a leadership framework designed for non-Native school leaders, comprising five foundational pillars: embracing Native educational sovereignty, decolonizing leadership practices, prioritizing Indigenous knowledge, adopting culturally affirming leadership practices, and engaging in authentic collaboration with Native stakeholders. This framework supports school leaders in making the necessary educational paradigm shifts to enhance both academic achievement and the preservation of Native students' cultural identity.

Below is a series of recent best-practice approaches aligned with this framework to help non-Native school leaders better serve their Native students.

Summary of Key Insights from Each Pillar

Embracing Native Educational Sovereignty

- Policy Advocacy: Advocate for educational policies at local and national levels that recognize and support Native sovereignty.
- Curriculum Development: Work with Native educators to create an inclusive curriculum that reflects Indigenous perspectives.
- Resource Allocation: Ensure sufficient resources are dedicated to programs that promote Native languages, cultures, and histories.
- Community Education: Organize workshops and seminars for the broader community, including non-Native educators and students, to raise awareness about Native sovereignty and its significance.

Decolonizing Leadership Practices

- Cultural Audits: Regularly perform cultural audits of school practices and policies to identify and remove colonial biases.

- Inclusive Decision-Making: Establish councils or committees that involve Native parents, students, and community members in school decision-making.

- Professional Development: Require staff participation in ongoing professional development focused on decolonizing education and understanding Native histories and cultures.

- Rewriting Narratives: Promote the inclusion of Native perspectives in all school communications, including newsletters, school board meetings, and public relations materials.

Prioritizing Indigenous Knowledge

- Indigenous Staffing: Hire Native educators and administrators to bring authentic Indigenous knowledge and teaching methods into the school.

- Collaborative Learning: Initiate exchange programs or collaborative projects with Native schools to enhance shared learning experiences for students and staff.

- Cultural Competency: Create a cultural competency certification for all staff that emphasizes Indigenous knowledge systems and their application in education.

- Indigenous Advisory Boards: Form an advisory board to oversee the integration of Indigenous knowledge into school practices.

Moving to Culturally Affirming Leadership Practices

- Cultural Celebrations: Organize regular cultural days or events led by the Native community to celebrate Native cultures and educate the public.

- Safe Spaces: Establish culturally safe spaces within the school where Native students can gather, share, and explore their identities.

- Responsive Pedagogy: Adopt teaching methods that are responsive to the cultural needs and learning styles of Native students.

- Empowerment Programs: Develop leadership programs for Native students that encourage them to assume roles of leadership within the school and community.

Authentic Collaboration with Native Stakeholders

- Community Forums: Conduct regular forums where Native communities can voice their needs, concerns, and visions for the educational system.

- Joint Initiatives: Collaborate on grants and projects that benefit both the school and the Native community, ensuring mutual advantages.

- Transparent Reporting: Maintain a clear reporting system to keep the community informed about school progress, challenges, and changes in educational practices.

- Continuous Feedback: Establish a structured mechanism for Native students and parents to regularly provide input on school operations and educational content.

The Urgency of This Call to Action

The need to adopt this framework is critical. Native students frequently encounter educational environments that fail to reflect their cultural identities or honor their communities' histories. This disconnect can lead to lower academic outcomes and a detachment from their cultural roots. By embracing these five pillars, non-Native leaders can help reverse these trends and foster the success of Native students and their communities.

Research-Based Best Practices

Preparing for Leadership

- Learn about the tribal communities served by the school.

- Engage in cultural competency training and develop mentorship relationships with Native educators and leaders.

First Day on the Job

- Approach with humility, prioritizing listening over imposing pre-existing beliefs.

- Involve Native staff and the community in expressing commitment to collaborative efforts.

Creating Long-Term Solutions

- Implement systemic changes that integrate Indigenous knowledge and practices into all aspects of school governance.

- Continuously assess these strategies based on feedback from Native students and their families, adjusting approaches as necessary.

- Ensure that systemic changes support the incorporation of all areas of school management.

- Regularly evaluate the effectiveness of these strategies by soliciting input from Native students and their families, and make adjustments where appropriate.

This call to action strongly encourages non-Native school leaders to adopt this leadership framework. The manner in which leaders guide their schools will ultimately determine the success of Native students, the representation of their culture in the school environment, and the support for Native identities. By adhering to these principles, non-Native leaders can impact their students' lives by bridging the gap between traditional education and Native communities. This effort goes beyond policy changes; it represents a long-term commitment to justice, dignity, and partnership. It is a call to action for all of us to step up as allies and shape the future of education in Native communities.

The Path Forward: Committing to Change and Continuous Learning

As non-Native school leaders, we must raise awareness and recognize that our roles extend beyond administrative duties; we also serve as advocates for Indigenous voices. Central to this commitment is the understanding that genuine change is not a destination. It requires adaptability, openness to feedback, and the courage to challenge entrenched inequities. Although this journey presents significant challenges, it is only the beginning.

A significant challenge is that systemic inequities have a profoundly negative impact on Indigenous communities. Addressing these issues necessitates a nuanced understanding of colonial history and its ongoing effects, which can be difficult for non-Native leaders to grasp fully. The legacy of mistrust and trauma within Indigenous communities poses a significant barrier to establishing authentic collaboration.

As leaders work to disrupt and dismantle deeply rooted practices that have perpetuated inequity for generations, they may encounter resistance from their institutions and the communities they aim to serve. This resistance can manifest as a reluctance to support new initiatives or engage in partnerships, making it essential for leaders to approach these challenges with humility and grace.

Committing to change and lifelong learning is fundamental to effective leadership and personal growth. This commitment involves more than simply acquiring new skills or knowledge; it is about dedicating oneself to ongoing development and understanding as the community and educational landscapes evolve. At its core, a commitment to change entails openness to reassessing existing beliefs, practices, and systems. Leaders must recognize that the status quo does not adequately serve all students, particularly Indigenous students. Acknowledging this reality is the first step toward fostering a culture of innovation and improvement.

Leaders must have the courage to question established norms and seek strategies that align with their communities' values, interests, and needs. This process can be uncomfortable, as it challenges deep-seated habits and beliefs. However, creating a more just and inclusive educational system is essential. Embracing the notion that personal and professional development is an ongoing journey means constantly seeking knowledge and skills; this journey does not conclude with formal education.

Leaders should engage in reflective practices, actively seek feedback, and remain open to new ideas and methodologies. By embracing lifelong learning, leaders develop the skills they need while modeling a culture of growth for their staff and students. This culture fosters an environment where all stakeholders feel empowered to learn, share knowledge, and collaborate on improvements. As leaders, you can inspire and empower your team, promoting a culture of growth and collaboration. Additionally, being an agent of change and a lifelong learner involves valuing partnership and community engagement.

Leaders should build a broad knowledge base that includes Indigenous communities' perspectives, ensuring that educational initiatives are relevant to the cultural contexts in which they are implemented. Change and learning within the community are ongoing, requiring deep flexibility, personal and organizational reflection, and responsiveness to community needs. This is not a task that can be completed and checked; somewhat off, it is a continuous process that demands commitment and determination.

The goal is to create spaces that prioritize growth and innovation, foster meaningful conversations, and recognize all voices. Strengthening teacher training is crucial for ensuring that leadership contributes to authentically equitable systems, providing all students with the quality education their communities deserve. Despite the challenges ahead, with a solid commitment to this work, non-Native school leaders can effectively support Indigenous students and communities.

Encouragement to Embrace Leadership in Native Spaces with Respect and Intent

Exemplifying dignified leadership in Native spaces is essential; non-Native school leaders must recognize their responsibility to use their influence within the educational system to amplify Indigenous voices. Central to this endeavor is educational sovereignty—the right of Indigenous peoples to govern their educational systems and cultural institutions. Leaders should advocate for policies that promote Indigenous self-determination and collaborate with local tribes to develop culturally relevant curricula and initiatives. Encouraging Indigenous students to explore their identities fosters empowerment in their education and instills pride in seeing themselves reflected in the curriculum.

In addition to supporting educational sovereignty, non-Native leaders must engage in the critical process of decolonizing leadership practices. This process involves a candid assessment of traditional leadership models that uphold colonial paradigms. Non-Native leaders should challenge hierarchical structures that marginalize Indigenous peoples and adopt more participatory approaches, creating space for Indigenous voices to be heard. This shift fosters a collaborative learning environment that acknowledges and respects Indigenous communities.

A key aspect of this commitment is ensuring that Indigenous knowledge informs leaders and guides the integration of Indigenous ways of knowing throughout the educational experience.

Non-Native leaders should collaborate closely with Indigenous elders and knowledge bearers to ensure that curricula are culturally relevant and teaching methods honor Indigenous traditions. By embedding Indigenous knowledge into the educational framework, we enhance the learning experience for Indigenous students, aligning it with their cultural beliefs while fostering mutual understanding and respect among non-Indigenous learners, ultimately enriching the school community.

Culturally affirming leadership practices that celebrate youth culture within schools further support students both inside and outside the classroom. Non-Native leaders must create an environment that honors Indigenous heritage through culturally responsive pedagogy, the celebration of Indigenous cultural events, and the integration of languages and traditions into daily school life. These practices not only engage students and boost their self-esteem but also cultivate a sense of community where every student can thrive.

Partnerships with Native communities should be grounded in collaboration, focusing on the strengths and resilience of the students and families served. Non-Native leaders must engage with Indigenous stakeholders, listening to and honoring their relationship with the land while acknowledging existing best practices in a non-commodified manner. Such partnerships should extend beyond mere consultation to include co-designing educational experiences that place Indigenous voices at the forefront. By fostering authentic relationships, leaders can enhance collaboration with Indigenous communities and create an academic landscape that is responsive and inclusive of cultural matters.

Ultimately, stepping into leadership within Native contexts is both complex and dynamic. By leveraging the five pillars of educational sovereignty, decolonizing leadership practices, embracing Indigenous worldviews in education, affirming youth culture, and engaging meaningfully with Native communities, leaders can create a more just educational experience for all students. This commitment not only addresses historical injustices but also contributes to a fairer, more equitable, and inclusive education system—one that allows every child to thrive within their Indigenous culture while honoring the diversity of Indigenous knowledge.

Appendix 1
Resources for Further Reading

Books

Indigenous Educational Leadership Through Community-Based Knowledge and Research

Editors: Robin Zape-tah-hol-ah Minthorn, Shawn L. Secatero, Catherine N. Montoya, and Jodi L. Burshia

Publisher: University of New Mexico Press (2025)

- This book focuses on Indigenous leadership identity, philosophy, and community leadership, emphasizing the empowerment of students through education.

Decolonizing Educational Leadership: A Critical Perspective

Author: Anne E. Lopez

Publisher: Routledge (2020)

- This work explores methods to decolonize educational leadership practices while highlighting the significance of Indigenous perspectives and sovereignty in academic settings.

Indigenizing Education: A Guide for Teachers

Author: Katerina A. Makarova

Publisher: University of Alberta Press, 2019

- This guide provides practical strategies for educators to integrate Indigenous perspectives and practices into their teaching, promoting culturally affirming environments.

Indigenous Knowledge in Global Contexts: Multiple Readings of Our Worlds

Editors: Susan A. Crate and Mark Nuttall

Publisher: Routledge, 2016

- This book examines Indigenous knowledge systems and their application in various global contexts, offering insights into how can they inform educational practices.

Culturally Responsive Leadership in Higher Education

Author: A. G. Terry

Publisher: Routledge, 2017

- This text discusses culturally responsive leadership in educational settings, focusing on understanding and incorporating diverse cultural perspectives, including those of Indigenous communities.

Critical Culturally Sustaining/Revitalizing Pedagogy and Indigenous Education Sovereignty

Authors: Teresa L. McCarty and Tiffany S. Lee

Harvard Educational Review, 84(1), 101–124 (2014)

- This article addresses Indigenous educational philosophies and practices, emphasizing cultural relevance and sovereignty. It introduces the framework of Critical Culturally Sustaining/Revitalizing Pedagogy (CSRP), arguing that

Indigenous education must not only sustain but also revitalize Indigenous languages and cultures, asserting that genuine educational self-determination is inseparable from sovereignty.

Toward Indigenous, Decolonizing School Leadership: A Literature Review

Authors: Khalifa, Gooden, Davis

Source: *Educational Administration Quarterly* (2019)

- This article synthesizes the literature on Indigenous and decolonizing educational leadership values and practices, drawing on both national and international contexts shaped by colonial schooling models.

Culturally Responsive School Leadership: A Synthesis of the Literature

Authors: Muhammad A. Khalifa, Mark Anthony Gooden

Source: *Review of Educational Research* (2016)

- This article reviews research on culturally responsive school leadership and outlines practical strategies for fostering inclusive environments that support Indigenous and other marginalized students. Khalifa, Gooden, and Davis emphasize the importance of affirming cultural identities, engaging families and communities, and implementing equity-focused policies to enhance student outcomes.

An Ecosystem of Knowledge: Relationality as a Framework for Teachers to Infuse Indigenous Perspectives in Curriculum

Authors: Maryanne McDonald, Sara Booth, Libby Jackson-Barrett

Source: *Asian Pacific Journal of Teacher Education* (2024)

- Using Design-Based Research, pre-service teachers engaged with relationality frameworks to rethink identity and cultivate authentic connections to Indigenous worldviews, thereby boosting their confidence and willingness to incorporate Indigenous perspectives into their teaching.

Possibility Not Difficulty: Difficult Knowledge in K-12 Classrooms as Opportunities for Renegotiating Relationships with Indigenous Knowledge

Authors: Velta Douglas, Fionna Purton, Danielle Bascunan
Source: *Alberta Journal of Educational Research* (2020)

- This article examines how educators engage critically with diverse student populations to incorporate Indigenous perspectives and knowledge in ethical ways.

Critical Culturally Sustaining/Revitalizing Pedagogy

Authors: Teresa L. McCarty, Tiffany S. Lee

Source: *Harvard Educational Review* (2014)

- This work discusses culturally relevant and responsive educational practices in Native American contexts, which are essential for creating an inclusive and supportive environment for Indigenous students.

Additional Resources

- Native Knowledge 360°: An initiative providing interactive teaching resources to help educators understand critical concepts and engage in pedagogy about Native peoples.

- First Nations Essential Readings List: A collection of key readings for those interested in the Native American experience.

- Indigenous Reads Rising: A platform offering best practice articles and resources for locating books by Native authors and illustrators.

- National Indian Education Association's (NIEA) Recommended Reading List: A curated selection of Native American children's literature endorsed by NIEA, tailored for K-12 education.

- "Native Ways of Knowing Book List": Compiled by the San Diego County Office of Education and California Indian Education for All to assist educators and parents in selecting high-quality Indigenous-authored books.

Appendix 2
Tools for Self-Reflection and Growth

Self-Reflection Tool for non-Native School Leaders

This self-reflection tool is designed around five key pillars: embracing Native educational sovereignty, decolonizing leadership practices, prioritizing Indigenous knowledge, fostering culturally affirming leadership practices, and engaging in authentic collaboration with Native stakeholders. Each pillar includes reflection questions and evaluation criteria to assist non-Native school leaders in their self-assessment and growth.

By regularly engaging with these questions and evaluation criteria, leaders can enhance their effectiveness as advocates for Indigenous students, communities, and educational sovereignty. Committing to this reflective practice will help ensure that their approach is respectful, inclusive, and aligned with the values of the communities they serve.

Pillar 1: Embracing Native Educational Sovereignty

Self-Reflection Questions:

1. How should I acknowledge and support Native communities' right to govern their educational practices?

2. In what ways have I advocated for policies that respect Native educational sovereignty?

3. Reflect on a recent initiative: How did it align with the principles of Native sovereignty?

Self-Evaluation Instrument:

- Rate your understanding of Native educational sovereignty on a scale from 1 to 5.

- Identify two specific actions you have taken to support Native educational sovereignty.

- Outline an area for improvement in embracing Native sovereignty and your plan to address it.

Pillar 2: Decolonizing Leadership Practices

Self-Reflection Questions:

1. What steps have I taken to identify and challenge colonial mindsets in my leadership approach?

2. How do I incorporate decolonization principles into my school's policies and practices?

3. Reflect on my decision-making processes: Do they prioritize Indigenous perspectives and values?

Self-Evaluation Instrument:

- Assess your progress in decolonizing your leadership practices on a scale from 1 to 5.

- List three specific changes you have made to decolonize your leadership.

- Develop a personal action plan for further decolonization efforts in the upcoming school year.

Pillar 3: Prioritizing Indigenous Knowledge in Leadership Practice

Self-Reflection Questions:

1. How can I actively incorporate Indigenous knowledge and perspectives into my leadership decisions?

2. In what ways have I facilitated the integration of Indigenous cultural content into the curriculum?

3. Reflect on my professional development: Have I pursued learning opportunities focused on Indigenous knowledge?

Self-Evaluation Instrument:

- Evaluate your prioritization of Indigenous knowledge in your leadership on a scale from 1 to 5.

- Identify three instances where Indigenous knowledge has influenced your leadership practices.

- Outline a strategy to enhance the integration of Indigenous knowledge in your school.

Pillar 4: Culturally Affirming Leadership Practices

Self-Reflection Questions:

1. How do I create a school environment that affirms and celebrates Indigenous cultures?

2. In what ways have I involved Indigenous students and families in shaping school culture and practices?

3. Reflect on my approach to discipline and behavior management: How does it align with culturally affirming practices?

Self-Evaluation Instrument:

- Assess your culturally affirming practices on a scale from 1 to 5.

- List three initiatives you have implemented that affirm Indigenous culture within the school.

- Identify one area for improvement in culturally affirming practices and your plan to address it.

Pillar 5: Authentic Collaboration with Native Stakeholders

Self-Reflection Questions:

1. How do I foster genuine partnerships with Native families, community leaders, and organizations?

2. In what ways have I actively sought input from Native stakeholders in school decision-making processes?

3. Reflect on a recent collaborative project: How did it reflect the values and needs of the Native community?

Self-Evaluation Instrument:

- Rate your effectiveness in collaborating with Native stakeholders on a scale from 1 to 5.

- Identify three partnerships you have developed with Native community members or organizations.

- Describe a plan to enhance authentic collaboration in the upcoming school year.

Appendix 3

Entry Plan Instrument for non-Native School Leaders

This entry plan instrument is designed to assist non-Native school leaders in developing a comprehensive entry plan that aligns with five key pillars: embracing Native educational sovereignty, decolonizing leadership practices, prioritizing Indigenous knowledge in leadership, culturally affirming leadership practices, and fostering authentic collaboration with Native stakeholders. Follow the steps outlined below to create an actionable entry plan.

Step 1: Preparation and Research

Directions:

- Understand the Community: Research the specific Native community your school serves, including its historical context, cultural practices, and current educational challenges.
- Identify Key Stakeholders: Compile a list of community stakeholders, including parents, elders, tribal leaders, and local organizations.
- Gather Documents: Collect relevant documents about the school's mission, vision, existing policies, and any previous community engagement efforts.
- Outcome: A foundational understanding of the community and its needs.

Step 2: Define Goals for Each Pillar

Directions:

- Set Specific Goals: For each of the five pillars, establish clear, specific, and measurable goals that you aim to achieve during your tenure, focusing on student success and community engagement.

1. Embracing Native Educational Sovereignty:

- Goal: Create a framework for integrating community governance in school decision-making.

2. Decolonizing Leadership Practices:

- Goal: Provide training sessions on decolonization for all staff members.

3. Prioritizing Indigenous Knowledge in Leadership Practice:

- Goal: Collaborate with local experts to integrate Indigenous perspectives into the

curriculum.

4. Culturally Affirming Leadership Practices:

- Goal: Initiate school-wide programs that celebrate Indigenous cultures and histories.

5. Authentic Collaboration with Native Stakeholders:

- Goal: Form a community advisory board composed of Native families and leaders.

Outcome: Clearly articulated goals aligned with each pillar.

Step 3: Engage with Stakeholders

Directions:

- Conduct Listening Sessions: Organize meetings with community members, parents, and students to gather their input on needs, hopes, and concerns regarding the school.

- Build Relationships: Focus on establishing trust and open communication. Be transparent about your intentions and commitment to serving the community.

- Document Feedback: Take detailed notes on discussions, noting recurring themes and specific stakeholder requests.

Outcome: A comprehensive compilation of community perspectives to inform your entry plan.

Step 4: Develop Action Steps

Directions:

- Create Specific Actions: Outline steps to achieve each goal defined in Step 2.

Example of Culturally Affirming Leadership Practices:

- Action Step 1: Organize a cultural celebration event in collaboration with Native families.

- Action Step 2: Develop a professional development workshop on culturally responsive teaching.

- Assign Responsibilities: Identify individuals responsible for each action step, including staff members, community partners, or yourself.

Outcome: A detailed action plan with clear steps and designated responsibilities.

Step 5: Establish Timelines and Milestones

Directions:

- Set Timelines: Establish realistic timelines for each action step, taking into account the school calendar and community events.

- Identify Milestones: Determine key milestones to assess progress, such as regular stakeholder check-ins or specific event and workshop dates.

Outcome: A timeline outlining the implementation of your entry plan.

Step 6: Implement and Monitor the Plan

Directions:

- Put the Plan into Action: Begin implementing your entry plan in accordance with the established timelines and milestones.

- Regularly Monitor Progress: Schedule regular check-ins to evaluate progress against your goals. Be flexible and adjust the plan as necessary in response to feedback and outcomes.

- Communicate Progress: Keep stakeholders informed about developments and progress. Share successes and challenges openly.

Outcome: Active implementation of the entry plan with ongoing monitoring.

Step 7: Reflect and Revise

Directions:

Evaluate Outcomes: After a designated period (e.g., the end of the school year), assess the success of your entry plan against the initial goals.

Gather Feedback: Request feedback from stakeholders on what was effective and what could be improved.

Revise the Plan: Based on your evaluation and feedback, update the entry plan to address any gaps and establish new goals for the upcoming year.

Outcome: A reflective process that promotes continuous improvement and deeper community engagement.

Appendix 4
Shared Decision-Making Model for Collaborating with Native Stakeholders

This shared decision-making model aims to ensure that Native stakeholders have a significant voice in the educational processes of predominantly Native schools. By incorporating their input at all levels of decision-making, this model promotes respect, collaboration, and empowerment within the school community.

Key Components of the Model

1. Inclusivity and Representation

- Diverse Stakeholder Groups: Form diverse groups comprising parents, students, educators, tribal leaders, and community members to represent a wide array of perspectives.

- Culturally Responsive Practices: Ensure that all processes are culturally sensitive and address the specific needs of Native stakeholders.

2. Structured Decision-Making Framework

- Consensus-Building Approach: Employ a consensus-building model to encourage collaborative discussions in which all voices are heard, and decisions are made collectively.

- Clear Roles and Responsibilities: Define stakeholders' roles in the decision-making process to ensure everyone understands their contributions and responsibilities.

3. Communication and Transparency

- Open Channels of Communication: Maintain transparency by holding regular meetings, forums, and digital platforms where stakeholders can share ideas and concerns.

- Feedback Loops: Implement mechanisms for ongoing feedback that allow stakeholders to express their opinions on decisions and suggest improvements.

4. Decision-Making Levels

- School-Level Decisions: Involve Native stakeholders in school policies, curriculum choices, and resource allocation through advisory committees.

- Classroom-Level Decisions: Encourage teachers to incorporate input from students and parents regarding classroom practices, projects, and learning materials.

- District-Level Engagement: Facilitate the representation of Native stakeholders in district-level discussions to influence broader policies affecting their schools.

5. Regular Meetings and Workshops

- Scheduled Collaborative Meetings: Conduct regular meetings with stakeholders to discuss ongoing issues, gather input, and make collective decisions.

- Workshops and Training: Offer workshops that equip stakeholders with the skills necessary to participate effectively in the decision-making process, focusing on leadership, advocacy, and cultural awareness.

6. Documentation and Accountability

- Record Keeping: Document discussions, decisions, and their rationale to ensure accountability and transparency.

- Public Reporting: Provide regular updates to the community about decisions made and their outcomes, keeping all stakeholders informed.

7. Evaluation and Reflection

- Assessing the Process: Regularly evaluate the effectiveness of the decision-making model by gathering stakeholder feedback on their experiences and sense of inclusion.

- Adapting the Model: Use evaluation findings to refine the decision-making process, ensuring it remains responsive to the needs and concerns of Native stakeholders.

Implementation Steps

1. Initial Stakeholder Meetings: Organize introductory meetings to explain the shared decision-making model and gather initial input from Native stakeholders.

2. Formation of Advisory Committees: Establish committees comprising Native stakeholders to guide specific areas, such as curriculum development, cultural programming, and community engagement.

3. Develop Decision-Making Protocols: Collaboratively establish protocols outlining how decisions will be made, including steps for gathering input, reaching consensus, and documenting outcomes.

4. Conduct Training Sessions: Provide training for all stakeholders in effective communication, negotiation, and cultural competence to enhance their participation in the decision-making process.

5. Implement Regular Review Cycles: Set timelines for reviewing the decision-making process, gathering feedback, and making necessary adjustments to ensure it remains effective and inclusive.

Appendix 5

Framework for Developing a School District Strategic Plan

This framework presents a comprehensive approach to creating a school district strategic plan, focusing on five key pillars of the leadership framework: embracing Native educational sovereignty, decolonizing leadership practices, prioritizing Indigenous knowledge, culturally affirming leadership practices, and authentic collaboration with Native stakeholders. The plan aims to promote equity, inclusion, and respect for Indigenous cultures within the educational system.

Step 1: Vision and Mission Development

Objectives:

- Establish a clear vision and mission that reflect the district's values and commitment to Native educational sovereignty and Indigenous cultures.

Actions:

- Engage Stakeholders: Conduct community forums and focus groups with Native stakeholders to gather input on the vision and mission.
- Draft Vision and Mission Statements: Create draft statements that encapsulate the district's goals and values.

Step 2: Assessment of Current Practices

Objectives:

- Evaluate the district's current practices in relation to the five pillars, identifying strengths, weaknesses, and areas for improvement.

Actions:

- Data Collection: Gather quantitative and qualitative data on current practices, policies, and stakeholder perceptions.
- SWOT Analysis: Conduct a SWOT analysis (Strengths, Weaknesses, Opportunities, Threats) focused on the five pillars.
- Community Surveys: Distribute surveys to parents, students, educators, and community members to understand their experiences and perspectives.

Step 3: Goal Setting

Objectives:

- Develop specific, measurable, achievable, relevant, and time-bound (SMART) goals aligned with the five pillars.

Actions:

- Collaborative Goal Development: Facilitate workshops with diverse stakeholder groups to brainstorm and prioritize goals.
- Pillar-Specific Goals: Identify at least two to three goals for each of the five pillars, ensuring they are interconnected and mutually supportive.
- Establish Metrics: Identify metrics and indicators to measure progress toward each goal.

Step 4: Strategic Initiatives and Action Plans

Objectives:

- Outline strategic initiatives and action plans to achieve established goals.

Actions:

- Identify Initiatives: Brainstorm initiatives that directly support each goal, and ensure alignment with the five pillars.
- Assign Responsibilities: Designate teams or individuals responsible for each initiative, and clarify their roles and expectations.
- Timeline Development: Create an implementation timeline that includes milestones and checkpoints to monitor progress.

Step 5: Resource Allocation

Objectives:

- Ensure adequate resources (financial, human, and material) are allocated to support the strategic plan.
- *Actions:*
- Budget Assessment: Review budgetary constraints and identify opportunities to fund initiatives aligned with the five pillars.
- Resource Identification: Identify additional resources needed, such as training, materials, or partnerships with local organizations.
- Funding Strategies: Develop strategies for securing funding, including grants, community partnerships, and fundraising events.

Step 6: Implementation

Objectives:

- Execute the strategic plan effectively while maintaining stakeholder involvement and communication.

Actions:

- Regular Communication: Provide stakeholders with updates on the initiative, progress, and celebrate successes.
- Professional Development: Provide training and professional development opportunities for staff, with a focus on culturally affirming practices and Indigenous pedagogy.
- Pilot Programs: Consider piloting initiatives in select schools or classrooms before district-wide implementation.

Step 7: Monitoring and Evaluation

Objectives:

- Continuously assess progress toward goals and evaluate the effectiveness of initiatives aligned with the five pillars.

Actions:

- Data Collection: Regularly gather data on established metrics to monitor progress and impact.
- Feedback Mechanisms: Implement feedback loops via surveys, focus groups, and community meetings to collect stakeholder input on the effectiveness of initiatives.
- Adjustments and Revisions: Use evaluation data to make informed decisions regarding adjustments to initiatives, resource allocation, and goals as needed.

Step 8: Reflection and Sustainability

Objectives:

- Foster a culture of reflection and ensure the strategic plan's sustainability beyond initial implementation.

Actions:

- Annual Review: Conduct an annual review of the strategic plan to assess overall progress, reflect on challenges, and celebrate achievements.
- Sustainability Planning: Identify long-term strategies for sustaining successful initiatives, including ongoing funding, training, and community partnerships.
- Continued Engagement: Maintain ongoing communication and engagement with stakeholders to ensure their voices shape the educational landscape.

Appendix 6

Sample School Board Policy Document: Consulting and Collaborating with Tribes

Policy Title: Tribal Consultation and Coordination Policy

Policy No: [insert policy number]

Date of Last Update: [Insert Date]

Purpose: This policy establishes formal processes to ensure that the needs and concerns of tribal stakeholders are included in decision-making through consultation and collaboration, as mandated by federal statutes and executive orders.

Scope: This policy applies to all schools and departments within the [School District Name] and serves as a guide for interactions and collaborations with tribal nations to address the unique educational and cultural needs of Native students.

Policy Statement: The [School District Name] acknowledges the significance of meaningful collaboration with tribal nations and is dedicated to fostering equitable community engagement practices throughout the district. This policy outlines specific areas of cooperation, such as education, cultural programs, and resource sharing, while emphasizing respect for tribal sovereignty and Native epistemology in shaping educational programs.

Key Elements:

Formal Agreements: The district will establish Memoranda of Agreement (MOAs) and Memoranda of Understanding (MOUs) with tribal nations to clarify the collaboration process, roles, responsibilities, and expectations for both parties.

Data Sharing and Confidentiality: Protocols will be developed to share student data, educational records, and other information while protecting the privacy and confidentiality of tribal members.

Professional Development: The district commits to providing ongoing professional development and training for school staff on bridging cultural gaps, implementing trauma-informed practices, and engaging effectively with representative groups and individuals from Native communities.

Monitoring and Sustainability: The district will regularly assess the effectiveness and impact of collaborative initiatives and programs, ensuring that relationships and efforts are sustained over time, irrespective of changes in leadership or personnel.

Systemic Change: This policy aims to create enduring systemic change, ensuring that the voices and priorities of tribal communities are consistently reflected in the design and implementation of educational programs and initiatives.

Implementation: The superintendent or designee is responsible for implementing this policy and ensuring that all district staff are informed about and trained on the processes and protocols outlined herein.

Policy Review and Amendments: This policy will be reviewed and amended annually as needed to reflect changes in federal or state law or the evolving needs of tribes and tribal communities.

Adoption: This policy was reviewed and adopted by the [School District Name] Board of Education on [Insert Adoption Date].

www.ingramcontent.com/pod-product-compliance
Lightning Source LLC
Chambersburg PA
CBHW061654120626
46550CB00003B/942